The Bulletproof Writer

Overcoming Constant Rejection To
Become An Unstoppable Author

A Guide For Newbies, Midlisters
& Best Sellers

By Michael Alvear

WOODPECKERMEDIA

Copyright © 2017
ISBN # 978-0-9977724-4-9

Table Of Contents

Section 2: The Fundamentals Of A Bulletproof Consciousness

Chapter Three
Developing A Higher Threshold For Failure

The most reliable predictor of success among the talented and creative is the sheer number of attempts at winning. This means you need a coping strategy for the inevitable rain of failures. We investigate how optimism is actually a lousy predictor of success and look instead toward cultivating what psychologists call an "Empowered self-explanatory style."

Chapter Four
Wired For Woe: How Our Brain Circuitry Undermines Resiliency & What We Can Do About It

Wondering why you gloss over 99 positive Amazon reviews and fixate on the lone negative one? Neuroscientists believe we are wired to perceive social rejection as a mortal threat. Learn proven ways to neutralize the brain's explosive reaction to rejection and how to build neural networks that form the basis of a bulletproof consciousness.

Chapter Five
Emotional First Aid: Managing The Pain Of Rejection

First we look at the power of the 48 Hour Sulking Rule and counter-intuitive strategies like "extinction" to move past the pain of major rejections. Then we look at cutting-edge strategies developed in just the last couple of years that show us how to manage emotional pain the way we do physical pain.

Chapter Six
Ruminations: Dealing With Rejections You Can't Seem To Get Over

Some rejections are so huge and life-changing we fall into rumination—intense brooding marked by obsessive thoughts that consume huge amounts of mental energy. Learn the three-step approach that performed better than talk therapies in academic studies.

Section 3: Looking Outward From A Bulletproof Perspective

Chapter Seven
How To Handle Critics, Criticism, And Bad Reviews

Discover how dozens of writers learned to deal with bad reviews —the insights they uncovered and the actions they take. Then we'll look at research showing bad reviews aren't a death sentence for your book, how they are often discounted by the public, and finally, nine healthy ways to inoculate yourself from their effects.

Chapter Eight
When Good Things Happen To Other Writers: Treating Poison Envy

Your friend's success isn't the cause of your envy; it's the trigger. Find out what experts believe is the real driver of a writer's jealousy and how to use that knowledge to heal yourself from the pain and anger. You'll also learn how to use envy as a change agent and how to tame the natural proclivity to compare yourself against other writers.

Chapter Nine
Taming The Biggest Critic Of All: YOU.

We need our inner critic because it's the CEO of Quality Control —it stops us from writing crap and getting publicly humiliated. But do we need its harshness and cruelty? Learn how a Nobel Prize winner's work on loss aversion can turn an inner voice of self-persecution into an inner consciousness of self-empowerment.

Chapter Ten
The Folly Of Trying To Learn From Your Failures

Studies show that trying to make sense of rejections or failures in an industry like publishing results in emotional chaos. Rather than learning from your failures we show you how to exploit them. With examples of how writers used their failures as paths to success you'll discover how to be emboldened not embalmed by dead-ends.

Section 4: A View Toward The Future

Chapter Eleven
At It For Years With Little To Show For It? Dealing With Chronic Frustration

A newbie who can't break in. A stalled midlister. A best seller sliding into irrelevancy. Years of frustration and disappointment have dug tunnels in your fortitude. How do you climb out of the vat of cynicism and despair? By getting clear on what drives all creative people and coming to an articulated conclusion that makes peace with years of roil.

Chapter Twelve
Radical Gratitude: A Counter-Intuitive Approach To Building Resiliency

Studies show the practice of gratitude is NOT particularly effective in calming us or making us more appreciative—at least the way most of us do it. However, using "counter-factual reasoning" in the practice of gratitude shows great promise in research settings. Learn about this fascinating technique and experience its wonderful effects.

Chapter Thirteen
Maintaining A Bulletproof Future

You can't go to the gym once and pop out muscles. You have to go again and again and again. So it is with building a bulletproof consciousness. This chapter serves as your maintenance regime—it contains all the key insights and action items you need to "do your reps" and keep in great mental shape for your journey in publishing.

Introduction

Maybe you're an unpublished author and received your 24th rejection letter.

Or maybe your first book just got a string of 1-star reviews.

Or maybe you're a midlister whose book signing attracted five people.

Or maybe you're a best selling author who got half the advance you expected because your last two books didn't do well.

Unpublished, newbie, self-published, midlister or *New York Times* best seller, ALL authors have to deal with constant rejection. It is an occupational hazard. It hangs over everything we do all of the time. What danger is to a cop, rejection is to a writer—always hanging in the air dripping with possibility. It is omnipresent and sometimes omnipotent. It reigns upon the talented and untalented in almost equal measure. It's a constant force both beginners and seasoned pros have to live with. And it is demoralizing, for the wins are few and far between and the losses big and packed like a pound of sardines.

Rejection comes at you from all directions—literary agents who won't take you on, editors who reject your manuscript, publishers who give you an insulting advance, anonymous reviewers who write hate speeches, and of course the ultimate rejection—poor sales. Somebody, somewhere at just about every stage of your writing life nails a NO to your forehead.

It would be one thing if you could just hang on, be willing to pay your dues and persist until you succeed. Surely then, rejection would wane and wither. But success, as any best selling author knows, doesn't protect you from rejection. In fact, it is precisely because you've experienced some success that rejection hurts even more than when you first started out. Partly because it triggers the "impostor syndrome" ("I fooled people into thinking I was talented and now I've been unmasked!") and partly because now you have more to lose from rejection.

For example, to a midlister rejection can mean getting a poor review by Publishers Weekly. But to a best selling author, rejection can mean getting a good review but not a *starred* one.

Rejection becomes infection when we internalize it, ascribe meaning it doesn't necessarily have and amplify it by taking on a chronically self-critical inner voice. We become the viral agent of the first blow and extend it through internal self-harassment. If you don't learn to deal with rejection in a constructive way it has the potential to destroy your writing career. It will make you think you're no good. It will make you question your worth. It will cause you to give up. It will give you writer's block. It will seriously compromise the quality of your writing. It can also throw you into fits of anxiety or depression.

I'm not going to throw motivational Band-Aids at you by using cutesy quotes or power slogans that'll keep you from quitting. I'm not going to pump sunshine up your ass to keep you inspired. I'm aiming for something much bigger than temporarily making you feel better or stopping you from a well-deserved crying jag or looking longingly at that bottle of Jack. My purpose for writing this book is to give you the insights and tools that will forever, and permanently, change the way you receive, interpret, act and react to rejection and criticism so that you can lead a calmer, successful, more satisfying and connected writer's life.

As a fellow author, I've experienced more rejection than any one writer could or should take. First, as a newbie trying to break in, then as a midlister and then even as a minor TV star. Here's how it went down: As a full time writer (nonfiction advice) my agent couldn't sell my last manuscript, even though I had written three books under legacy publishers and starred in a reality show that aired in 12 countries including the U.S. on HBO.

Then the recession hit and the floor went out from under me. I spiraled into a depression. Bills mounted. I lost my health insurance. I bounced around. I drank a lot. I packaged my work into small ebooks and sold it off my blogs as downloadable PDF files. I generated some revenue but all it did was slow my descent.

I put three of these ebooks on Amazon. They tanked. I fell into a deeper depression. I had to borrow money from my parents. My humiliation was complete. After a decade of writing I faced complete, abject, *ruinous* rejection. My agent abandoned ship. Publishers didn't want my work. And the public refused to buy my self-published works.

This is the part where I'm supposed to give you my inspiring half-time speech in which I dig deep and roar back as a bloodied but unbowed champion. That's not quite how it happened. My comeback (I now make six figures annually as an author) had nothing to do with "psyching myself up," pulling myself up by my bootstraps or any of the typical clichés associated with redemption stories. Yes, I worked hard. Yes, I had a lot of discipline. Yes, I persevered.

But so did all the writers I hung out with before the Great Recession. Not one of them is still writing, even though by any objective standards they had more talent than I did.

I succeeded because I developed a mental toughness that helped me transcend the kind of constant rejection that other writers, *better* writers, could not. In this book I'm going to show you how I developed a bulletproof consciousness so that you have a better shot at breaking into publishing if you're a newbie, staying in it if you're a midlister and prospering more if you're a best seller.

Rejection itself has no meaning except the closing of a particular door at a particular time. The meaning of the event is strictly up to interpretation and that brings us to the central problem we'll tackle in this book:

The obstacle in front of us isn't as difficult as the obstacle inside us.

While you have no power to reverse a rejection, you do have the power to reinterpret its meaning so that it doesn't leave you gutted. It's possible to greet bad news with a *consciousness of self-correction not self-persecution.* I'm going to show how to do that by introducing you to the powerful and often surprising strategies uncovered by the latest studies in resiliency—strategies that were so effective in building my own bulletproof consciousness. For example: How to stop bad reviews from reducing you to a puddle. Or how to stop poor sales from convincing you that life is over.

We do not have absolute control over our responses to adversity but we do have a major influence. We can significantly increase the likelihood of a constructive reaction to a negative event by cultivating resilience and personal hardiness. We will build strength out of diversity by building a skill set and turning it into applicable wisdom.

In the movie *The Matrix*, Keanu Reeve's character Neo faces secret service agents with powerful guns. Morpheus, the captain of the spaceship, cryptically tells Neo that he can overcome their attacks. Neo asks, *"Are you saying I can dodge bullets?"* Morpheus replies, *"No, Neo, I'm saying when you're ready, you won't have to."*

In other words, the bullets don't exist as physical objects. They exist in his mind. "Dodging" the bullets (a famous scene in the movie) is a sign of Neo's slowly-awakening consciousness but it still anchored him to an untruth. Why is he dodging bullets that don't exist? As Neo's consciousness grew he went from dodging bullets to letting them pass through him unharmed.

This is my goal: To transform your definition of rejection's bullets so that you can do what Neo did—let them pass through so that you feel the breeze but not the contact.

It's possible to become a bullet-proof writer—the kind that acknowledges bad news without being crippled by it. The kind of writer that doesn't judge her worth by the number of rejections she gets but by the way she handles them to move forward. The kind of writer that processes rejection in realistic but empowering ways—without denying its pain or consequences but without falling into rumination and self-blame. The kind of writer that bounces back easily from stress, rejection, criticism, alienation, hopelessness and despair.

I am going to teach you how to *turn poison into medicine.* The kind that promotes calm and confidence so that you can get to the real work at hand—letting your words make a mark on the world.

Chapter One

The Nature Of Publishing Makes It Hard For Writers To Build Resiliency

Publishing is one of the few industries that systematically rejects its most talented people. To understand the scale of how badly it misjudges talent you only have to glance at how many times publishers rejected writers like William Faulkner, Vladimir Nabokov, Marcel Proust, Gertrude Stein, Jack Kerouac, and John Le Carré. The list is endless and entirely accessible—just Google "famous authors who've been rejected."

It's difficult to fully grasp the enormity of the industry's inability to recognize talent until you compare it to other industries. Imagine Samsung, Sony or Verizon rejecting Steve Jobs' resume with a form letter.

Or Goldman Sachs, JP Morgan Chase, and Citigroup telling Warren Buffet he doesn't have what they're looking for.

Or Google, LinkedIn and Pinterest telling Mark Zuckerberg they see no future for him in social media.

It would never happen. Yet rejecting talented authors happens regularly in publishing. Brilliant writers like Stephen King, J.K. Rowling, Ursula Le Guin have amassed so many rejection letters they could build a bonfire and keep a lot of us warm for a week.

In almost all other industries people generally rise to the level of their abilities. Gifted with numbers? You'll get a great job in accounting. Talented in physics? You'll land a high paying job in aerospace. Adept at design? You'll step into a high-powered ad firm.

But publishing? Not true. Demonstrably not true. Maxwell Perkins, often described as the greatest literary editor (he edited Hemingway, Fitzgerald and Thomas Wolfe), passed on William Faulkner. According to the New York Times, novelist and literary critic Malcolm Cowley once wrote to Faulkner, "In publishing circles your name is mud. They are all convinced your books won't ever sell."

Alfred A. Knopf, the house noted for its literary quality, passed on Herman Hesse. Many of the best loved novels on your bookshelf have a tortured history of rejection. Harcourt Brace Jovanovich refused J. D. Salinger's *Catcher in the Rye*.

The founder of Grove Press, Barney Rosset, hated J.R.R. Tolkien's *Lord of the Rings*. The New York Times quoted him as saying it "Was not credible. I thought I recognized Nordic figures from mythology, but it seemed a mishmash to me. I couldn't follow it, literally couldn't finish reading it."

Nan Talese, Houghton Mifflin's executive editor, passed on Salman Rushdie's *Midnight's Children*, which ended up winning the prestigious Booker Prize.

These are just some of the outrageous rejections of the most talented among us. Who knows how many more there have been, since most rejections are private affairs. If that's the way publishers treat the top 1% how are they treating undeveloped talent, or talent on the verge of realizing its potential or talent that has no representation?

Is Rejection An Indictment Of Your Work?

Yet no matter how many times we read about famous authors who were repeatedly rebuffed, we writers cement ourselves to a demonstrably false belief: Rejections are an indictment of our work. Despite the long list of rejected authors who (and I say this with love) are way more talented than you and I are, we believe things like "If I were talented I wouldn't get rejected" or "If my work was any good publishers would flock to it."

It may very well be true that your work sucks but it's just as true that other considerations may have caused your rejections. Timing is a big one ("We just got through launching a similar book").

So is "fit" ("We don't really publish books in this genre").

So are market trends (if you sell salt in a market looking for pepper, it doesn't matter how good you made the salt).

So is editor preference ("I just don't like this type of writing").

So is publisher skittishness ("Your last book tanked so it doesn't matter how good your new manuscript is, we're not taking a chance on you again").

So is a publisher's confidence that it can sell it ("It's a great book but I don't think the market will understand it").

So is a publisher's backlist ("Love LOVE your book but we've published too many like it).

And so is an editor's skepticism that she can sell it to her associates ("I adore this book personally but the committee has rejected too many books like it for me to pitch it").

My point: There are dozens of reasons for rejection other than the quality of your work.

This mindset—that rejection is a reflection of our worth—prevents us from overcoming adversity. After all, if you agree that rejection means you're a lousy writer then there's no point in trying to overcome adversity.

The confounding thing about publishing is that you often don't know why you get rejected. And because we don't, because few in publishing are willing to explicitly state the reason for their rejection we are left with a haunting suspicion—but not absolute certainty—that we are failing because we're untalented (or talented but peddling unwanted wares).

This is the existential question most of us writers find ourselves asking—are we getting rejected because we're no good or because of other factors beyond our control? This self doubt is toxic, and in a great many cases flat-out inaccurate. I'm going to show you how to deal with self-doubt in the next chapter. For now, I just want to identify it as a central challenge in a writer's life.

Why Do Editors Write Fabulous Rejection Letters?

If you're a midlister-to-best-seller you've probably noticed that many of your rejection letters sound almost as complimentary as acceptance memos. I personally have received rejection letters that read like starred reviews from Publishers Weekly—until the last "thanks but it's not right for us" line. What's up with that? Why not just decline politely without the excessive compliments?

First, it's a way editors cover their asses against the potential embarrassment of passing on a book that later becomes a blockbuster best seller. Yes, she rejected the book but look at that rejection letter! Clearly, she recognized the talent! It's a way of softening the perception of a bad decision.

Second, it would be a self-destructive move to alienate an author's agent with a stinging critique, no matter how legitimate, because that agent may bring them a best seller in the future.

You're The Exception To The Rule...In Your Imagination.

We cannot truly move forward without addressing a hope that will not die—that you'll be an instant hit if you're a beginner, a latent hit if you're a midlister or a bigger hit if you're a best seller. Admit it, you feel that way. I know I did when I first started out. Still do and I've been writing full time for fourteen years. I constantly fantasize that whatever book I'm currently working on,

THAT'S the one that hits the New York Times bestseller list and catapults me into a life of champagne and cocaine.

Almost everybody believes that they will be "The One"—the author that hits a homer the first time at bat, or every time he's at bat. And even when you mouth the platitudes of hard work and acknowledge how difficult it is or will be, you still hang on, in the dark crevices of your longing, to the idea that the Gods will smile upon you and elevate you above the great unwashed.

And why shouldn't you feel that way? Everywhere you look there are massively successful authors. In fact, you almost never see failed authors. Part of your delusion (and mine) is backed up by your sensory intake. The only writers you see or read about are the successful ones. There is no *New York Times* Best Seller List Of Failed Books. *Publishers Weekly* does not review unimportant or poorly written books. *The New Yorker* doesn't profile unpublished authors. Amazon doesn't list books ranked #101-1.8 million in any of their bestseller lists.

Our victories are public; our losses are private.

In other words, there is MASSIVE FAILURE out there. A COLOSSAL amount of writers whose books don't sell, get reviewed or get listed on any Amazon list. But you don't see them. The only thing you see are successful writers, writers who ARE on the top 100 lists, authors who do get profiled, and writers who bathe in starred reviews.

You never see struggling authors unless you're having lunch with them.

To fully understand our "perception bias" you need only look at a big industry that doesn't have it—Sports. Most athletes don't suffer from the kind of magical thinking that writers do because there are constant displays of public failure. In publishing, you hardly ever see public displays of loss. In sports you see it every time you go to a stadium, turn on the TV, click on your smartphone or raise the volume on the radio. In sports, loss is inevitable, ubiquitous, constant and again, *public*. And that's a big reason athletes are far more realistic about their chances of success than writers.

The lottery business is about the only industry that generates as much perception bias as publishing. Their ads do not showcase people who lost. The media do not interview people who bought the wrong ticket. And because they don't, winning seems easy, widespread and inevitable. It's the same with writers. Everywhere you look, you see enormously successful authors. Everywhere, with almost no exception. So the net effect of this illusion, this perception bias, is that success is easy and there's only reason you haven't achieved it: You're no good.

The perception bias that affects writers can best be described as a zoo that exclusively contains albino rhinos. In the absence of other experiences, it's natural to think that there must be a lot of albino rhinos out there in the wild. But in reality they are a genetic mutation rarely seen in the animal world. Remember this and you'll always be able to put your chances of massive success in its proper context: *Whenever you see a writer that hit it big you are essentially seeing a white rhino.*

What Are The Odds Of Making It As A Successful Author?

First, we need a definition of success. I'm going to assert a definition I think most of us can agree on: Producing work that adds value to readers, generates respect and admiration by our peers, fulfills our sense of purpose and earns us enough money to ensure our prosperity.

Now, what are the odds of you making it as a successful writer in the way I've just defined it? High? Medium? Low? You probably guessed low.

You have no idea how low "low" can go.

Research expert, sociologist and novelist Dana Beth Weinberg did an interesting analysis on QueryTracker.net, a free service that provides a database of agents and publishers and tracks the timing and success of manuscript queries. Here's what she wrote in her blog:

> *"QueryTracker has over 73,000 author subscribers and lists close to 1300 agents. At the time of publication the website boasted over 1200 "success stories." Imagine a hat filled with the names of all of the authors signed up on the site (73,000), and of those, 1200 are chosen by agents for acceptance while the rest are rejected. In this thought experiment, the flat odds of matching with an agent—never mind bestsellerdom—are less than 2%; the average author could expect, all things being equal (which of course they are not), to be rejected more than 98% of the time by agents.*

In real life, the odds are even worse, especially since not all agents are looking for authors at any given time and since authors submit multiple projects to multiple agents, thus increasing the pool of queries and projects to accept or reject among a fixed number of agents and publishers.

In a recent conversation, agent April Eberhardt told me that she has about twenty clients and receives more than six thousand queries a year. At most, she only has the capacity to take on a handful of additional authors for representation, making it necessary, she says, to reject perfectly good or even great queries and manuscripts. Another agent told me her agency received over 40,000 queries in a year and only had 40 clients total."

What Percent Of Authors Make A Living Wage?

If you think the odds of getting an agent is depressing, wait till you see the odds of earning money. In order to do the math the first thing we need to know are the number of authors out there. Here's what New York Times best selling author Dominic Smith wrote in themillions.com:

"The real answer is that no one knows exactly how many novelists are at work in America. We can guess and infer and extrapolate. The truth is that no one's ever asked the question of the U.S. population in any organized way. There's never been a "novelist" box to check on a tax form or on a state agency survey. After studying the data, I'm inclined to think there's a million people writing novels, a quarter of a million actively publishing them in some form, and about 50,000 publishing them with mainstream and small, traditional

presses. Then again, I have a novelist's penchant for rounding numbers for the sake of narrative convenience. Putting the numbers aside, what we do know is that there's an army of folks writing novels— some bad, some glorious— against staggering odds. Writing a novel is like starting a small business and investing thousands of hours without knowing exactly what it is you're going to end up selling. It's a leap of faith every time, even for someone who is five novels into a career. Can we agree on a low-end pool of 250,000 active novelists? If I had to account for all the people writing novels that will never see the light of day, in either self-published or published form, I'd put that number at one million."

Let's go with Smith's "low-end pool of 250,000 active novelists." Now we need an estimate of writer incomes, which you can get from authorearnings.com. Guess how many of us writers make a living wage (considered to be around $50,000/year)?

Two thirds of us? A half? A quarter?
Keep going.

30%? 20%? 10%?
Keep going.

5%? 3%? 1%?
Keep going.

Oh, for God's sakes! Who can count that low?
The answer: About one half of 1%.

According to authorearningsreport.com, in their definitive study of author earnings in 2016, 1,400 authors out of approximately 250,000 make a living wage of $50,000 a year or more. I encourage you to read the report, as it breaks down income between authors at the Big Five, small and medium publishers and those who self-publish.

The good news, if you can call it that, is that nearly 4% of authors make $10,000 or more. But is that glass half full or half empty? Because that means 96% of all authors make less than $10,000 a year. Actually, it's worse than that: Around 60% of all authors make less than $1,000 a year.

More Prozac, Please

By now you should feel like a suicidal dyslexic about to throw herself behind a bus. Writers are up against a lot. We cannot talk about managing the emotional impact of constant rejection without first addressing the challenges I've outlined here. Indeed, it's imperative that you absorb three facts about the publishing industry:

1. Rejection Is Most Likely Not An Indictment Of Your Work.

Clearly, a lack of talent (or *enough* talent) is a factor in whether you get rejected or accepted, but it is not the only one. And if you look at the difference in talent between the writers who got rejected and the ones who "made it," maybe not even the main one. In the next chapter, I will propose a strategy that will help you move forward with a belief crucial to your resiliency—that you write things worth reading.

2. You Will Not Be Spared The Wrath Of Rejection.

Barring the equivalent of a lightning strike, you will not be an instant hit. And even if you are, you will still face massive rejection (ask any author who wrote a hit and couldn't duplicate it). It is one thing to be hopeful and optimistic, it's another to delude yourself with the magical thinking that you and you alone will be spared the slings and arrows of rejection. The truth is you're going to get cooked like a kipper. I say this not to discourage but to prepare you. Knowing the laws of gravity shouldn't stop you from jumping out of an airplane; it should cause you to look for a parachute.

3. Less Than 1% Of Writers Make A Living Wage.

Again, I present the odds not to spray Buzz Begone on your aspirations but to illuminate the facts so that you can build resiliency. There's no need to build grit if success is easy but it isn't. The odds are overwhelmingly against you. As you'll soon see, that's not a reason to avoid getting in or staying in publishing but it is a reason to plan accordingly.

These three fundamental facts should fill you with an odd mixture of despair and...comfort? The despair speaks for itself, but the comfort might take some explaining. You see, recognition of the facts, not ignorance of them, can lead to equanimity and self-composure in a number of ways.

Despair comes easily when you *wrongly* believe that you're getting rejected because you have no talent. But if you know that the majority of your rejections have nothing to do with your talent, well, that's...*comforting*, isn't it?

Depression sets in fast when you *wrongly* think you will be spared the rejection that most writers experience. But if you know that writers you respect face constant rejection, well, that's... *reassuring*, isn't it?

Despondency rises exponentially when you make little or no money from your writing and you *wrongly* perceive that a great many authors do. But if you know that one half of one percent actually make a living wage, well, that's...*a relief*, isn't it?

Toiling under false assumptions breeds self-persecution. Working in the light of truth can liberate you from the bonds of self-blame and help you chart a new course for success. Which we are about to do in the next chapter.

Chapter Two

Preparing For A Bulletproof Consciousness

Joseph Campbell once pointed out that entrances to some ancient Japanese temples were "guarded" by 26-foot Nio Statues carved with one hand welcoming you and one hand warning you away. Campbell theorized that it represented a way of weeding out the immature and unready while welcoming the courageous willing to test themselves for greater glory. Writing is like that. There are two Nio statues guarding the temple of publishing with an explicit message: *Do Not Enter Without The Expectation Of A Painful Journey That May Or May Not End Joyfully.*

The Bulletproof Consciousness does not take that warning lightly. It does not enter the temple without first understanding what is in store and preparing for the ego-threatening obstacles that guard the treasure.

As you pass the Nio Statues and enter the antechamber of publishing's temple you'll notice two things. The first is that it is crowded with writers just like you trying find the treasure. In fact, it's China-crowded. So crowded you actually can't see a path to the treasure. It looks like a hundred rock concerts just let out in Beijing. "No wonder I get so many rejections," you think to yourself, "Look how many authors I'm up against!"

The second thing you notice is how many bullets are flying around. It's a constant spray from all angles, hitting just about everyone. Some people collapse to the floor immediately, others stagger and look for cover. You look down and see lots of the fallen (they quit writing) but you also see some writers who go about their business and the bullets don't bother them at all, even when they take a whole cartridge. We'll come back to them in a minute.

The next thing you notice is a fantastic, endless view of an African savannah where white rhinos bask in watery success. Look left and you'll see miles of white rhinos signing books with lines that wrap around the horizon. Look right and you'll see more white rhinos driving up in their Mercedes, flying to their second homes, taping TED talks, bedding beauties, jetting to Davos, marrying royalty, talking with Terri Gross, appearing on The Daily Show and counting endless stacks of cash.

You, of course, along with the throngs of concert-goers, make a move forward to join them by sending in manuscripts, talking to your agent, or if you're self-published, releasing a book. But you're prevented from walking into the savannah by an 18-foot thick acrylic glass panel. Those white rhinos aren't a mirage, they're just on the other side of a spotlessly transparent wall. And a curious thing happens every time you—or anybody—tries to walk, climb or in any way touch the glass wall by offering a manuscript, asking for a blurb, requesting a higher advance, or hoping for a starred review: It fires bullets of rejection. The bullets come as letters, emails, phone calls or conversations rejecting whatever it is you were going for.

The more you try to walk into the savannah to join the white rhinos and claim your piece of the pond, the more the wall sprays you with bullets. You see a newbie send manuscripts to 24 different publishers and get shot 24 different times. You see a midlister trying to convince her editor about a new book idea and you hear the spring mechanism in the gun. You see a self-published author waiting for the first sale to somebody he's not related to and you hear a shot ring out.

There are writers trying to break into the business, writers who've been in it for a while, even writers who once hit it big and are trying again. Some are unpublished, some are self-published, some have small indy publishers and many have major publishers.

You talk to some of the veterans in the antechamber and they'll tell you how incredibly hard it is to get into the white rhino'd savannah. Some have come close and tasted the nearby fruit. Some—especially women—have even gotten to the top of the wall only to find that it's topped by a glass ceiling.

It's A Jungle In There

The place is so packed that you see every type of writer—even former white rhinos like John Berendt (*Midnight At The Garden Of Good And Evil*) and Joseph Heller (*Catch-22*), authors who wrote one stellar book that defied the laws of gravity and whose subsequent books crashed like meteors capable of wiping out dinosaurs.

Everyone there is pushing and shoving, trying to get into the savannah. Some writers help other writers get closer and they get rewarded; some help and get stabbed in the back. Some posers try to get in with white rhino costumes while others who clearly have white rhino genes get pushed to the back because...because... well, no one has actually figured out the because. These are authors admired by the white rhino cognoscenti and frequently dubbed "a writer's writer" for their exquisite prose. Authors like Mavis Gallant and Fernando Passoa, who should have been rubbing butts with the other white rhinos but didn't because talent alone is insufficient for entrance.

The machine guns run 24/7 and the chorus of "Ow!" "Hey, that hurt!" And "I should have listened to my parents!" is often pierced by horrific howls of pain, no doubt caused by publishers who gave insulting advances, championed lame book titles, proposed disastrous covers or simply decided not to publish a book even though they paid the advance and the writer spent half her life writing it.

Luck Is No Lady

Amid the cries and screams of worthy writers screwed by the system, suddenly the glass wall parts, clearing a path to the savannah. A slight mist descends, paralyzing everyone in their place, except for a shy, 22-year-old young woman who ambles forward with her hand over her mouth, crying with joy, unbelieving that she, a first-time novelist who never went to university or even took a creative writing class, gets to skip the line and take her place among the fatted royalty. As she steps into the savannah she magically turns into a white rhino and waddles over to the feast.

Suddenly, the glass walls shut, the paralyzing mist disappears and witnesses start shouting. "Hey! Unfair!" shouts one writer. "I've been working my ass off and this skinny bitch just waltzes in without taking a single bullet?"

"This is bullshit!" shouts a writer with eight books to her name under a major New York publisher. "How in God's pajamas, can somebody with no experience, write a piece of shit and leapfrog over the rest of us working stiffs?"

On and on you hear the complaints and the grumbling and this is your first lesson in the Temple of Publishing. In fact the lesson is printed right above you on a 24 x 24 foot sign that you inexplicably missed as you walked under it: *ABANDON YE ALL HOPES OF FAIRNESS.*

Three Questions To Ask Yourself

Now that we've had a taste of what the writing landscape looks like, let's back up to the gates of publishing's Temple. The bulletproof consciousness, upon seeing the Nio Statues and the gravity of its warning/welcome understands it must answer three questions before it is prepared to undertake the journey:

1. Should You Go Into (Or Stay In) An Industry With Almost Zero Chance Of Success?

I gave you all the depressing income data and the odds of making it in the last chapter not to discourage but to give perspective. These are terrible odds. *Horrible.* But they're not a reason to avoid publishing if you're a beginner or to get out of it if you're a midlister.

Famed software engineer Leo Polovets (Google, Linked-in), a performance thought leader, advises that we "separate the decision from the outcome" when we exercise choices that are inherently risky (like going into, or staying in, writing). Here's what he said:

> *"Let's say I propose the following game: you pay me a dollar, I flip a coin, if it's heads I give you $10 and if it's tails you get nothing. This is a great bet for you to take, but of course you will walk away with nothing half of the time. The key is to remember is that you made the right decision, even though it did not lead to the ideal outcome. Making good choices is all you can ask of yourself. For example, let's say that if you ask for a raise, perhaps nothing happens 2/3 of the time and you get a 10% salary bump 1/3 of the time. So you ask your boss, and he says no. That sucks. But did you make the right decision? Sure! You had nothing to lose, and you knew that asking was not a sure bet. Your correct decision didn't pay off this time, but it might pay off the next time or the time after that. Why would you be unhappy about making the right choice?"*

How This Applies To Writers

We can make the right decision without getting the desired outcome. The lack of a desired outcome doesn't mean we made the wrong decision.

Buried in all the bad news about the odds of success is a counter-intuitive insight that can help forge greater resiliency: If the odds are astoundingly low, there's no reason to feel bad about rejection.

See, the pain of rejection is proportional to your expectations. If you expect success to be easy (80% of writers make $100,000+!) then rejection will feel like a sandpaper bowel movement. If you expect it to be hard (less than half of 1% make a living wage) then you anticipate lots of rejection as a matter of course.

Having a better understanding of what you're up against helps you process rejection better. If the chances of "making it" were good, then you *should* feel bad about a rejection because it *would* be an indictment of your work. But if the chances of success resemble winning the lottery then you shouldn't feel anywhere near as bad about rejection.

Take a good, hard look at the numbers I posted in the last chapter. Are your expectations in line with the facts? If a friend decided to make it in an industry where less than 1% earn a living wage would you tell them to expect a little rejection or A LOT?

The bulletproof consciousness walks into the Temple knowing it has a 99.5% chance of failure so it isn't surprised when rejections come at it like a band of angry baboons. Now, there is a second question you must answer before walking past the Nio Statues.

2. Why Are You Writing?

Nietzsche once wrote, "He who has a why to live for can bear almost any how." If you get in touch with *why* you write you can better suffer the slings of writing's how.

Since most writers don't make a lot of money I am assuming that you write for something other than cash. Most of us don't write because we like to; we write because we *have to*. There is an inner force propelling us toward self-expression, to tell stories, to communicate with our tribe.

But there's also another major reason we write: To create value. This is a fortuitous reason as almost all philosophers, psychologists, psychiatrists, clergymen, mystics and new thought leaders believe that a key to happiness is in creating value for others, which enhances our self-esteem and creates a sense of purpose.

For me, as a nonfiction advice writer, my mission has always been to start a conversation. To make people think. To make you laugh. To solve desperate problems. In other words, my purpose, my mission is in creating value for people. I seriously believe that and it seriously changes my reaction to rejection. When I forget my purpose I react to a rejection by thinking, "My work is terrible. I'm a hack and this rejection is proof of it." When I remember my purpose I think, "It's a shame that my ability to make people think, laugh and solve problems won't be manifested in this particular way but there are always other possibilities even if I don't know what they are at the moment."

Admittedly this is a lot easier to do as a nonfiction advice writer but it applies to fiction writers too. And if you don't believe that I would like to explain what happens to readers when they pick up your books: It can make them laugh so hard they forget their problems. It can entertain them so intensely that everything bad in their lives disappears for a few hours. It can arouse curiosity and introduce novelty. It can fill their lives with beauty. It can make them think outside their own walls and build a world that doesn't exist to explain a world that does.

In other words, writing is the equivalent of giving readers a bouquet of flowers. If your purpose is to gift those flowers, does it really matter which publishing house pots the flowers? Does it matter how much they pay you to deliver them? Does the design of the pots matter? Does it matter that some reviewers will hate the flowers and others will love them?

Yes, some of these details are important but they're important in the sense that they multiply the effect you want; they don't create it. *You* create it. More money for the flowers is nice, but the amount won't *replace* the essence of flower-giving.

The point is that once you understand your sense of purpose, your ability to face, process and overcome rejection rises exponentially. In the face of the greater value delivered, the obstacles raised by rejection are put in perspective.

If you're having trouble identifying what value your writing delivers, what mission is worth dedicating yourself to, this list will help whether you're a fiction or nonfiction writer:

Value Propositions Writers Can Deliver

- Inspire
- Entertain
- Educate
- Illuminate
- Right a wrong
- Make people laugh
- Help others survive, thrive and achieve
- Add to the store of human knowledge
- Protect and preserve things like values, environment or culture
- Give joy and pleasure to others
- Lead
- Provide knowledge and wisdom
- Solve problems
- Deal with breakups
- Absorb deaths
- Unbottle emotions
- Understand the human condition
- Verbalize issues buried by silence
- Open hearts and souls
- Release frustration
- Accompany people in their journey
- Let go of pain

- Express feelings
- Call attention to problems
- Work out insecurities
- Introduce alternative ways of thinking
- Create peace and understanding
- Voice new ideas or approaches
- Open up possibilities
- Express alternate visions
- Heal
- Ease deeply buried pain
- Unearth fresh new feelings
- Get through raw places
- Expose people to alternative ideas and thinking
- Decant the soul
- Make sense out of the senseless
- Define speechless moments
- Say goodbye
- Understand ourselves
- Understand each other
- Map the human condition
- Express the intangible
- Explore issues neglected in modern society
- Call attention to the neglected
- Kindle reflection, introspection and clarity

- Stand for what has no voice without us
- Preach the virtues and vices of love
- Understand the world around us and inside us
- Communicate the importance and weight of the darkness in our souls
- Reassure that we're not alone
- Discover the secrets of our existence
- Bear witness
- Speak truth to power

Look at that list! If you don't believe that you can contribute something that's on there, it's time to quit (or never start). Still, it's possible to feel like the value you provide is weightless because of your limited success. Here you have to remember your place in the writing cosmos. To quote Whitman: "The powerful play goes on and you contribute a verse." Ours is not to own the play but to help it move forward. What is your verse? That is the question. Your answer, and the depth to which you feel it, is essential in forging the kind of resiliency required if we are to pass under the Nio Statues with any hope of surviving the journey.

I promise if your purpose for writing is to make a lot of money you're going to encounter the same giant boulder coming at you that Harrison Ford did in *Raiders of The Lost Ark*, only it's going to make a pancake out of you.

If your purpose is to gratify your ego with glowing reviews from people you've never met you may as well stick your hand in the meat grinder right now for all pain it's going to cause you.

I promise if your purpose is to see your name in lights and get your calls answered by important people, success will ignore you like a well-fed cat.

The only thing that will help you survive the journey is the inner force that propels you to tell stories, add value and contribute a verse. Let me repeat that in a different way: *The bulletproof conscience is anchored by first understanding and then standing on our stated purpose for writing.* The more we hold that vision in our minds—what verse we add to the powerful play—the better writers we will be, the more resiliency we can build and hopefully, the more success we will have.

Now, let's tackle perhaps the most difficult question you must ask before passing under the Nio Statues.

3. Is Your Writing Good Enough To Enter The Temple?

As stated before, one of the confounding things about publishing is that you never know if you're getting rejected because you've got the talent of a tick on your dog's privates or because of factors that have nothing to do with the quality of your writing.

Newbies, did that agent reject you because your writing is so bad the spellcheck feature declined to inspect your manuscript or did the agent just have too many writers on his roster?

Midlisters, was the POV on the manuscript you couldn't sell that bad or did your editor already sign a similar book?

Self-published authors, were those awful sales a function of an amateurish story or did you just simply market the book badly?

The point is that there is no objective way to know why we've failed. You cannot enter Publishing's Temple (or stay in it) without having a plan to deal with this profoundly central question: *Is rejection an indictment of your work?*

Make An Informed Bet

The truth is you can't answer that question. You're better off making a bet with yourself, instead. I call it the Writer's Wager— that it's in your best interest to behave as if your writing is worthy, since publishing's record of judging talent is so bad it outweighs any advantage of believing otherwise.

So, a crucial step in developing a bulletproof consciousness is committing to the Writer's Wager. This does not absolve you of improving your craft through writing groups, classes, retreats, seminars and more. Nor does it mean that you should not consider changing what you write or the way you write if enough trusted, informed opinions suggest you do. But the Wager says you *have to* proceed as if your work is worthy of publishing and selling or there's no point in carrying on. I don't know of anybody who proudly stated, "I know my work is shit but I overcame massive resistance to it so that I could deliver it to a unappreciative public."

No, there is only one reason to overcome adversity—because we have something worthwhile to say through our writing. You have to BELIEVE that there is a place for your work in the canon or you may as well throw in the towel, paint yourself into a corner and throw away the key, if I may mix my metaphors.

Getting Ready To Pass Under The Nio Statues

You understand that the Nio Statues guarding Publishing's entrance aren't kidding when they say you're welcome to come in as long as you're prepared to endure a world of pain for the tiniest *possibility* of success. You've faced the three main questions that all writers must answer before their journey begins: Why go into an industry with a 99.5% failure rate? What is your mission? Is your writing good enough to enter the Temple?

You understand you will face an avalanche of obstacles, challenges and rejections for your entire career, not just the beginning or the middle of it. You agree that market factors, not your worth as a writer, will account for the vast majority of the rejection you'll face. You see right through the perception bias most of us have about "white rhinos"—that mega-success happens all the time to a great many people. We know that society only allows us to see the mega-successful and that it distorts our ability to accurately assess our chances and misleads us into blaming ourselves the way a regular rhino might blame itself for not having the sense to be born with a genetic abnormality.

You have a clear view of your stated mission, the 'verse' you add or intend to add to Whitman's "powerful play." You understand that your mission, your purpose is the real fuel that powers your desire to write and that everything else—including white rhino success—are terrific add-ons that are desirable but not critical.

You've shed the fantasies, accepted the reality, anchored to your mission and committed to the Writer's Wager. NOW you are ready to go past the Nio Statues. NOW, you are prepared for the hydra-headed beasts that await (agents, editors, publishers, reviewers, internet trolls and every manner or person that can make writers miserable).

And as you step into the initial darkness you are comforted not just by your new ascendant consciousness but the absolute knowledge that you're taking this journey not because you're certain you'll succeed but because not striving for your mission is unacceptable.

Chapter Three

Developing A Higher Threshold For Failure

As you go deeper into the Temple's catacombs you see a fellow-traveler who's about to put his hand on the glass wall, the one that fires bullets at every writer's attempt at success. You try to stop him. "Wait! That's going to hurt!" you yell. But he ignores you and something odd happens—bullets spray out in loud bangs but they don't hurt him. In fact, he doesn't seem to hear them and they don't slow him down for a second. He is completely immune to them. And because he is, he finds ridges, cracks, fissures, crevices and holes in the glass wall that were not apparent to you and mounts it with the dexterity of a seasoned rock climber.

Meet the midlister.

"Hey Mr. Midlister!" you yell. How come the bullets didn't stop you?"

"Oh!" he exclaims. "Don't let the scary sound or the look of the bullets scare you. With the right mindset, you'll see they're nothing but heat-lightning—scary-looking but harmless. I haven't felt the pain of these little buggers in a long time."

Clearly, this has given Mr. Midlister a significant advantage. He can actually climb the wall and you can't even get near it without the "anticipatory anxiety" of getting a bullet in the forehead. You see him climb, burrow, jump, crawl, walk, run and dive with gusto.

Apparently the wall is actually a series of dimensions and the deeper you go in, the more money, food, drink and fun there is. Mr. Midlister may not be in the savannah, but he's clearly found a place between nowhere and the promised land. He seems happy, respected and relatively prosperous. You want some of that so you ask him how he did it.

Deconstructing The Delusion

"The first step," he says, "is to grab a helmet over there and never take it off." You look over and see rows and rows and rows of augmented reality helmets. You never noticed them before but now you realize that some—not many—but some of the hundreds of thousands in the crowd are actually wearing them. And the ones wearing them seem to have gotten very deep in the wall, as Mister Midlister has.

"Why the helmets?" you ask.

"They help you see rejection for what it is," he says. "So your threshold for rejection, rebuffs, dismissals and obstacles rises exponentially, allowing you to focus on your work, which in turn, helps you succeed."

You grab a helmet and examine it. You feel the outer hard shell and the impact-absorbing liner. There's even a comfort liner and vent to keep you comfortable. You see the retention strap that keeps it on you, but what really fascinates you is the visor. It has this weird, computer-generated sensory input with sound, video, graphics and even GPS data. "Don't let the sophisticated patterns on the visor fool you," yells the midlister from a point high above you. "It's just a simple bullshit detector that can distinguish the simple act of a door closing from your interpretation of it as a career-ending event."

In fact, that helmet allows you to see the truth about rejections—they're not bulk ammo designed to destroy you. They're simply a representation of a shut door.

"Whoa!" you think. "This helmet can take me places I never thought I could go." So you put it on and an amazing thing happens. As you send out manuscripts or pitch a book idea to an editor or discuss an advance with your agent, every rejection comes at you like bullets do to Neo on *The Matrix*. At first you dive for cover. Then you duck, dodge and weave. And finally, you allow them to pass through you, realizing that they never had the deathly meaning you had always ascribed to them.

So let's talk about that helmet. Or rather, how you can interpret a rejection the same way the helmet does without actually having to wear it.

Success *Requires* Rejection

Eminent psychologist Dean Simonton, the researcher who wrote the seminal book on success and creativity—*On The Origins Of Genius* (Oxford University Press, 1999)— once said, "Creativity is a probabilistic consequence of productivity." Translation: Success comes down to the number of attempts made on its behalf.

Simonton studied creative geniuses in many fields and made some eye-opening discoveries. For example, the best predictor of winning a Nobel Prize in science is the rate of journal citation. How do you get a citation if journals routinely reject studies for publication? *With a lot of submissions.* How do you conduct a study that yields results worth publishing in a journal? *With a lot of failures.*

Simonton's research shows that people who succeed are not necessarily smarter or more creative than their peers—even in fields that <u>require</u> you to be smarter than average. For example, he found that people in mathematics and engineering with an IQ of around 120 found "success" at much higher rates than people with much higher IQs.

But if the trophy doesn't go to the smartest or most talented, then who does it go to? According to Simonton, the ones with a higher threshold of failure. In fact, one of the most surprising results of his research seems counter-intuitive: The successful experience more failure than the unsuccessful!

Failures Are Precursors To Success
In Simonton's view, once there is a "floor" of talent or intelligence (say, an IQ of 120 in engineering), success can be predicted by the sheer number of attempts at the goal. It's a product of the law of large numbers. Tonnage. The more ideas we have the more likely we are to come up with good ones. The more attempts at

solving a problem the more likely we'll solve it. In other words, the more editors you contact the more likely you'll get a publishing deal. The more attempts at riding the bike the more likely you'll pedal away. The more books you write the more likely you'll end up with a best seller. Simonton discovered that a larger number of tries *usually* results in a larger number of successes.

I'm emphasizing "*usually*" because Simonton's research didn't show that perseverance alone was a guarantee of success, but the factor that most differentiated it from failure among the highly intelligent, creative and talented.

Simonton basically makes an empirical case for the old proverb, "If at first you don't succeed try, try again." But with a couple of caveats. You can't keep doing the same thing over and over again. That's not the definition of being insane, it's the definition of being unimaginative. Simonton did not say that the successful were the adequately talented who <u>merely</u> persevered; he said success most frequently came to the adequately talented who persevered in many different and sometimes radical, ways. So be careful when somebody advises you to "keep at it." They should really be saying, "Keep at it but try different approaches."

If success is, as Simonton's research proved, a "probabilistic cons-equence of productivity" then it makes sense that the successful have a coping strategy for failure that the unsuccessful don't. In other words, they metaphorically put on that helmet Mister Midlister told you about earlier. The one that allows you to see rejection's bullets for what they are—a simple NO.

Not "No, because you suck." Not "No, therefore you should quit." Just a simple NO. As in, not at this time, not at this place and not for these people.

A Coping Strategy For The Rain of Failure

Elizabeth Gilbert, the author of the megahit, *Eat, Pray, Love,* credits a lot of her success to the coping strategy she developed:

> *"Whenever I got those rejection letters I would permit my ego to say aloud to whoever had signed it: "You think you can scare me off? I've got another 80 years to wear you down! There are people who haven't even been born yet who are going to reject me some day—That's how long I plan to stick around.*
>
> *I decided to play the game of rejection letters as if it were a great cosmic tennis match: somebody would send me a rejection, and I would knock it back right over the net, sending out another query that same afternoon. My policy was: you hit it to me, I'm going to hit it straight back out into the universe."*

Clearly, Mister Midlister, like Elizabeth Gilbert, has a higher consciousness about rejection. In order to understand how he processes it you first have to understand he had to give up the notion that you probably live under right now—that acceptance is the only antidote to rejection. In other words, you think the solution to a problem is to remove the problem.

Let's say the love of your life broke up with you. You're

heartbroken. In your mind, the only possible solution to the end of your emotional pain is to get back together. But your partner has moved on and that is not going to happen. If getting together is the only possible solution to your heartbreak you are in big trouble. Certainly that may be the solution you PREFER, but it is not the only solution available.

You could meet someone else for example. You could, over time, realize that you don't need someone to make you happy. You could come to realize that your partner was actually stopping you from accomplishing important things in your life, and now is the opportunity to act on them.

Mister Midlister knows if the only acceptable solution to heartbreak is resuming the relationship, we would never date or get married again and he applies that to writing. If the only acceptable solution to a rejection is acceptance from the people who rejected him, he'd have a very short writing career.

Reversing the rejection and gaining acceptance may be our *preferred* way of resolving the problem but it's hardly a viable one. In publishing, a "rejection event" is pretty much permanent. If an editor rejects your manuscript she will not re-read it. If a critic gives you a bad review, he will not re-write it.

Mister Midlister understands that the solution to a permanent problem is not attempting to remove its permanence but to extract its benefits. That could come in the form of new insights, different approaches or more nuanced tactics. It's essentially about finding a way to create value from rejection, to use it as a catalyst to change us into more resilient beings.

In other words the problem of rejection isn't solved when it disappears. It's solved when it no longer makes you suffer.

The Case For Drowning Optimism In The Bathtub

Mister Midlister didn't get as far as he did with positive thinking. He believes that optimism, in the way most Americans practice it, is hollow and unhelpful. It tries to paint over bad news with a smiley face. It pretends the closed door isn't locked. It thinks you don't have to fix the brakes if you make the horn louder. Positive thinking elevates *seeming* over being. It has no place in building resiliency and the quicker you get rid of it the better off you will be.

If optimism isn't the answer, Mister Midlister knows cynicism isn't either. It too has all the markings of optimism but in darker shades. Both are completely different world-views yet they create the exact same result—hazy thinking based on little evidence.

If not optimism or pessimism, then what? "Empowering Attribution." To understand it, we need to acquaint ourselves with what psychologists call "explanatory styles."

Why Did You Fail?

How do you explain the causes of your failures? Do you see them as malleable or immutable? Ultimate success may depend on your answer. If you see the causes of your failures as unchangeable then it will be hard to find a way around the barriers you've encountered. If you see them as changeable then you'll motivate yourself to find a work-around.

Psychologists suggest there are two kinds of "self-explanatory styles"—empowering and disempowering. Let's use this example to see the differences: The rejection of a manuscript the editor described as "poorly written."

Self-Explanatory Style	Reaction To Rejection	Is The Cause Of Your Failure Malleable Or Immutable?	How You Might Proceed
Empowered	"I'm a lousy writer"	Malleable	"I can improve my writing by going to more workshops."
Disempowered	"I'm a lousy writer"	Immutable	"There's no point in trying to improve because writers are born, not made."

Notice that in both cases the reactions are the same—"I'm a lousy writer" but the causal explanations are miles apart. Who is more likely to conquer adversity in this scenario? Who is more likely to investigate options and follow up on them?

Notice this has nothing to do with positive or negative thinking. You can be an optimist and think the cause of failure is immutable. There are a lot of optimists in the Midwest's "Tornado alley." The ones likeliest to survive the tornadoes are the ones who think their plight is malleable ("What can we do about this?") and leave town. The optimists most likely to die think their plight is immutable ("It's God's will") and stay.

Your goal shouldn't be to improve your temperament but to cultivate an empowering self-explanatory style. Let's make a distinction between temperament and attribution with this example: You're in a barn and you step in horseshit. What are the different reactions you can have?

	Scenario
Optimist	"There must be a pony in here somewhere."
Pessimist	"There are no ponies in here and I'm never going to get this shit off my shoes!"
Disempowered Attributionist	"There's no point in cleaning this up because if I stepped in one pile there must be lots more."
Empowered Attributionist	"Why is this shit here and are there bags I can get rid of it with and a mop to eliminate the stink, and maybe a big clay pot of flowers to replace the stain on the floor."

Cultivate An Empowered Self-Explanatory Style

Drowning optimism in the bathtub doesn't mean you should start wearing pessimism's new clothing line. "Staying positive" is important because mood is important. You're a lot easier to live with if you have a sunny disposition. Ask your friends. But "staying positive" isn't really helpful in dealing with rejection. It's a nice sheen, I'll give you that, and certainly better than having a negative luster, but as a weapon? The Nio Statues would laugh if you walked past them into the nine-headed hydra armed with what amounts to a butter knife.

Optimism is a desirable outlook. It is not a desirable strategy.

Psychologists know that people who rely on their optimism too much—"positive thinkers"—tend toward overconfidence and carelessness. They have short planning horizons and think a winning smile and a confident attitude can overcome lack of preparation, discipline and focus. Think about the Great Recession. It wasn't just greed that caused it. Optimism blinded us to disaster ("The housing market is going up, up, up! Don't bring me down with your negativity!") and denied reality ("The stock market isn't overheating—quit being a wet blanket!").

In writing, optimism can create a false sense of your own skills. Why go to a writing workshop? You're a terrific writer! What could they possibly teach you?

As Mister Midlister gradually let go of both optimism and cynicism, his consciousness adopted a system of Empowering Attribution so that he saw the causes of problems as malleable not immutable. This avoided the paralysis of cynicism and the obliviousness of optimism so he could craft an appropriate response. And with this new consciousness he didn't see rejection as something that shouldn't be there, but as something he had to deal with. He no longer sees rejection the way Neo in *The Matrix* first saw bullets—as something that could maim or kill. Now, he sees them as something that doesn't have to stop him from his goals.

Turning Knowledge Into Wisdom

Now that we know that rejection has no electrical charge, no organic, fundamental way of hurting us, we can just move on, right? Not so fast. Our relationship to rejection is much like the relationship that somebody with an anxiety disorder has to their feared object. Yes, they may understand *intellectually* that there is nothing to fear but they've grooved a response pattern that's hard to break.

The next step is knowing how to handle your emotions when the rejections inevitably come. If you're like most writers, you've grooved a unique response pattern that intellectual knowledge alone cannot break.

So let's break it.

Chapter Four

Wired For Woe:
How Our Brain Circuitry Undermines Resiliency & What We Can Do About It

Developing a bulletproof consciousness requires us to accept the limitations imposed by our biology. And there is no greater limitation than the way our brains are wired to greet bad news.

As we discussed earlier, rejection has no organic power to hurt you. The pain it has is the pain you grant it. The solution is simple—stop granting it power—but that's harder to do than it sounds. It's not that you're weak, stubborn or unwilling. It's that you're biologically wired to perceive rejection as a mortal threat. We even language it that way. Rejection can make you say, "It feels like something died in me," or "I feel like I've been stabbed."

To understand why so many of us overreact, let's visit with neuropsychologist Rick Hanson and his book, *Hardwiring Happiness: The New Brain Science of Contentment, Calm, and Confidence.* Hanson has been studying the brain for the last couple of decades. He, along with other researchers, have discovered that the brain has a built-in negative bias that gets easily "highjacked by alarm."

Wired For Woe

Humans are about 2 million years old. As European homo sapiens we are 40,000 years old. But as humans living in the "modern world?" Probably about 5,000 years old. And that's giving the definition of modernity a wide latitude, for it includes Antiquity, Medieval and Modern ages.

Hence the brain has been evolving for 2 million years but less than one quarter of 1% of that evolution occurred during the past 5,000 years of "Modern life." If the brain's timeline were condensed to a year, it would have been evolving itself for cave-man danger from January 1 to December 30. It would've started evolving to modern life stressors on December 31.

Clearly, the brain has not evolved itself to the every day stresses of contemporary life. We're essentially using a Stone Age brain to deal with modern-day threats. Is that a lion jumping out of the bush or a rejection letter from a publisher? Doesn't matter—sound the alarm, flash red, start running.

Here's Hanson on why it was so important for the brain to wire itself to negativity:

> *"Imagine being a hominid in Africa a million years ago, living in a small band. To pass on your genes, you've got to find food, have sex, and cooperate with others to help the band's children (particularly yours) to have children of their own: these are big carrots in the Serengeti. Additionally, you've got to hide from predators, steer clear of Alpha males*

and females looking for trouble, and not let other hunter-gatherer bands kill you: these are significant sticks.

From a survival standpoint, sticks have more urgency and impact than carrots. If you miss out on a carrot today, you'll have a chance at more carrots tomorrow. But if you fail to avoid a stick today - WHAP! - no more carrots forever...

Consequently, your body generally reacts more intensely to negative stimuli than to equally strong positive ones. It was a matter of life and death to pay extra attention to sticks, react to them intensely, remember them well, and over time become even more sensitive to them. Consequently, the brain evolved a built-in negativity bias. It continues to operate inside us today as we drive in traffic, head into a meeting, settle a sibling squabble, try to diet, watch the news, juggle housework, pay bills, or go on a date. Your brain has a hair-trigger readiness to go negative to help you survive."

Hanson's theories on the brain's evolution (in line with general consensus among researchers) are based on physical evidence of the brain's structure along with imaging studies. For example, the brain produces more neural activity when it is exposed to negative stimuli than equally intense positive ones. Negative stimuli are also perceived faster and easier. Studies show that people can identify angry faces faster than happier ones even if the images are shown so quickly that it isn't possible to have conscious recognition.

In addition, the amygdala, sometimes described as the brain's alarm bell, or threat assessment region, uses about two thirds of its neurons to look for bad news and react quickly to it. It stores and experiences negative events quickly and vividly and positive events slowly and ephemerally. These facts led Hanson to a memorably-phrased observation:

> *The brain is like Velcro for negative experiences but Teflon for positive ones.*

Our negativity bias shows up everywhere. Studies show that humans generally learn faster from pain than pleasure. People work harder to avoid losing $100 than to gain it. Painful experiences are more memorable than positive ones. It takes on average, five good interactions in a relationship to make up for a single bad one.

As Hanson states, *"The brain is good at learning from bad experiences, but bad at learning from good ones."*

The built-in negativity bias also explains why strong dislikes are easier to acquire than strong likes. An undesirable character trait is more easily remembered than a desirable one. An insult cuts more than a compliment lifts. Trust is easier to lose than to gain. It is easier for a vice to hurt a hero than a virtue to help a villain.

As Hanson states, *"Negative contaminates positive more than positive purifies negative."*

How Does This Affect Writers?

The brain's structure explains why you will gloss over fifty great Amazon reviews and obsess over the single negative one. It explains why you concentrate on the parts of the story your editor wants to change rather than the parts she wants to keep, even though she's thrilled with 90% of it. It explains why you motivate yourself with cruel rather than kind self-talk. You are wired to store, remember and react to everything that happens to you in publishing with a built-in negative bias.

How Depressing! Should We Give Up And Throw Our Computers In The Pool?

Hardly. There are proven methods of rewiring the brain to counter its negativity bias. We're going to get to those in a moment. First, we need to understand what's happening to us, for there is power to that understanding. A lot of us writers feel like we're weak, or immature or flawed in some way because we over-react and feel so easily defeated by rejection. But the truth is you and I don't have a character flaw; we have a brain that processes perceived threats in unhelpful ways. And it's further exacerbated by the fact that we work in an industry over-populated with roaring lions, poisonous snakes, fire-breathing dragons, and flesh-eating Pterodactyls.

And I'm only talking about the editorial assistants.

Ironically, the seeds of a solution lay in acknowledging how powerless we are in the face of our biology. Biology may dictate our first response but as you'll soon see, not the second, third or fourth. Through insights, exercises and strategies, we can not only change our minds but rewire our brains to react in calmer, more helpful ways.

But before we get to that point we need to understand why our Stone Age brain treats the rejections we writers get with nearly the alarm it does to physical danger.

Et Tu, Rejection?

Studies have shown that people rate rejection as a more emotionally painful experience than disappointment, frustration or fear. We can feel the sharp point of rejection even with strangers who don't mean anything to us. Consider the famous "ball toss experiment." You and two strangers are waiting in a lobby to take a test. One of them starts tossing a ball. They toss it to you, making you feel included. But the two are not strangers—they are researchers and after the first wave of ball tossing they exclude you and toss the ball only to themselves.

How do you feel in that situation? A couple of strangers you don't care about decide they don't want to toss the ball to you. Would you be upset? Would you feel rejected?

This study has been replicated many times and yielded pretty much the same results—subjects report significant emotional pain from being excluded. Their mood shifted downward and they experienced a noticeable drop in self-esteem. Now, how could something so trivial trigger such sharp emotional pain?

You might wonder if a low self-esteem or lack of confidence might be to blame. Or perhaps a tendency toward co-dependency. But experts in the highly interdisciplinary field of neuroscience (biology, psychology, medicine and more) make a different case and it's a powerful one. In his book, *Your Brain At*

Work, David Rock interviewed thirty leading neuroscientists. This is their general consensus: The brain often treats social rejection as gravely as survival threats because it sees them as related. In our evolutionary past being rejected by a social group, a tribe, could mean as certain a death as being cast into a pit of venomous vipers.

Being cast out of the group meant you no longer had easy access to food and water, companionship, nor a social system that helped your children survive. Fitting into a social group was so critical to survival that the brain evolved to pick up the slightest change in your status. The people who couldn't pick up early signs of danger got kicked out of the tribe and probably died. The ones who developed an ear for the subtleties of the tribe's rules and customs were able to better maneuver and stay in the tribe's good graces, ensuring their well-being.

Staying in the tribe was a matter of life and death so the brain developed an early warning system to look for danger signs. To make sure you paid attention, it poked you with distress in the form of fear and anxiety. It triggered sharp pain at even the slightest snub lest it become a pattern that could lead to being "voted off the island," where you would die a slow, horrible death without even a decent shot of tequila.

How Does This Relate To Writers?

Your brain treats rejection as a sign that you're about to get kicked out of a life-giving tribe. In this case, a publishing tribe filled with agents, editors, and respected peers that offer all the resources you need to survive—money, respect, prestige and admiration.

This is where your conscious mind and the structure of your brain diverge. The conscious mind thinks, *"Oh, for heaven's sakes, it's just a rejection letter."* But your brain, "highjacked by alarm" sees that letter as a symbol of the tribe casting you out, ostracizing you, leaving you to the hungry wolves.

That's why midlisters and best sellers suffer the most from rejection. The newbie is trying to get into the tribe, which comes with its own set of miseries, but the midlisters and best sellers? They're *in* the tribe. They get all the benefits—royalty checks that pay the bills, requests to speak in front of groups, respect from peers and access to higher-ups to accelerate further success. They see their names on the best seller lists. Doors get opened for them assuring them of more money, more resources, more ability to survive and thrive. When rejection threatens their status in the group (in the form of bad reviews, books that tank, editors no longer so interested in their new ideas, smaller advances), the writer's brain can react with a code red terror warning level.

From that standpoint, every rejection represents a social threat. Public criticism in the form of reviews lowers your status in the tribe ("Poor Alyson, she's just not as good as her first book. Maybe she doesn't belong with us.") Editor indifference can threaten your livelihood ("If an editor that likes my work passes on it, what chance do I have of selling it to somebody I don't have a relationship with?"). The list goes on. You start fearing that while you're not out the door, you're inching closer to it.

Logic And Common Sense Don't Do Much To Calm The Fight-Or-Flight Brain.

When scientists told participants in the ball tossing experiment that the game was rigged to elicit just that type of negative feelings it didn't do much to alleviate their pain. In one group scientists told the subjects that the ball tosses were from members of the loathsome Ku Klux Klan and even THAT didn't seem to help.

Essentially, we are hard wired to experience emotional pain when we are rejected—no matter what it's about or who's doing the rejecting.

The Nature Of Writing Exacerbates The Negativity Bias.

We are not selling vacuum cleaner parts made in China. We are gifting a part of our souls. This makes rejection that much more personal and difficult to accept. You can always rationalize that a buyer didn't need parts, but how do you rationalize that they didn't want YOU?

Your writing is an extension of yourself. It's your imagination, your thoughts, your feelings, your sweat and tears. There is no part of your "product" that was made outside of your heart and soul. We are emotionally invested in our writing in ways that we are not with our jobs or hobbies. Gustave Flaubert once said about books, "Drops of our heart's blood are visible in the characters of our writing."

You put everything into your work so any judgment of it— whether it's an agent who won't take you on, an editor who rejects your concept or an audience that won't buy your book—feels like a judgment of you as a person. Worse, it feels like your contribution to Whitman's "powerful play," your "verse" got stamped with a "NOT WANTED" sign visible from the space station. So, on top of your Stone Age brain acting as if the zombies have scaled the outer walls of your compound, you also have to contend with what can feel like a primal abandonment of your work.

The Nature Of Publishing Deepens The Negativity Bias.

The nature of publishing accelerates the brain's propensity toward being "highjacked by alarm." Rejection is widespread in publishing, affecting everyone at one time or another. There is a daily wall, a blizzard of rejection visited upon those who pass the Nio Statues into the temple. However, we do not see the thousands of other writers who also received a rejection letter, a bad review or an insulting advance the same day you did. There is only one email in front of us and it has our name on it. Until social media does a live feed of all the other writers facing rejection the day we do, we will never appreciate that rejection is the rule not the exception. So we personalize it and draw false conclusions about our talent or our worth with the aid of almost no evidence.

How Depressing! Should We Just Quit?

Put down the application for Wal-Mart greeter. There isn't just hope; there's hope on stilts. Author and humorist Ashleigh Brilliant once described a vexing issue by saying, "I don't know the solution but I admire the problem." That's where we start—by admiring the problem. Neuroscientists greatly admire the way the brain has set itself up, and through their appreciation they've come up with solutions you will find quite advantageous not only in your writing career but in all aspects of your life.

Let's take a look.

You Are Hereby Relieved Of Self-Blame

Upon "admiring the problem" one comes to an obvious conclusion: Our reaction to rejection isn't a sign of weakness, fragility, stupidity, low-esteem, co-dependency or a lack of grit or determination. It is a reflection of the way our brain evolved to help us survive. Whew! And here you thought you were just a namby-pamby, overly-sensitive, candy-assed milksop who needed spine enhancement surgery.

It isn't you. It's your brain.

And once you realize that you can stop adding to the biology of your problem with the psychology of your judgment. No amount of raised esteem, strength or smarts is going to overcome your brain's wiring. Out of the bondage to our wiring comes a new freedom—permission to stop the self-judgment, self-blame and self-harassment that compounds the problem.

If a false alarm goes off in your house a lot of things happen. The dog jumps, your ears pop, the cops come and you get slapped with a false alarm fee. But the one thing that doesn't happen is self-blame. Why? Because you know it isn't your fault. It's the faulty wiring. The system got tripped and it can only respond in one way—with flashing lights and ear-splitting noise.

It's the same with your brain. Get a rejection? It sets off false alarms. Now, have you ever tried to stop a false house alarm by talking to it logically, pointing out its inconsistencies and gently persuading it to lower its volume? Then you know how ridiculous it is to use the same approach with the false alarms your brain sets off.

You don't shut it off with words, you do it with actions that slow the neural storm. The brain triggered the alarm because it thinks you're about to be cast out of the tribe. What if you could show your brain that you are in fact, well connected to other tribes that help you survive and thrive? Like your friends, your family, people that love and cherish you. Or your employer, clients or partners who help put food on the table and pay the bills.

Connect To Your Tribes
Scientists have identified a loss of belonging as central to the pain of rejection. What is the antidote to a perceived disconnection? More connections. And that's why it's so important to attach yourself to your tribes when rejection comes a-knockin'.

The single worst thing you can do to fight the neural onslaught triggered by social rejection is to isolate and pretend nothing happened. All you're doing is proving to the brain that it was right—you're cast out, alone, with no one to count on. It's just a matter of time before the dingo eats your baby. It will sense that danger is getting closer and increase the neural firing that creates even more distress.

If you get a letter of rejection, a phone call declining a guest spot on a morning show or a bad review, you should pick up the phone and talk to a friend or family member. And if you're really feeling bad, make plans to be with someone or, preferably a group (you know, a TRIBE) for lunch coffee or dinner. Studies have shown that the pain of rejection decreases *significantly* when you reach out to friends or family. Why? Because the feeling of connection calms the electrically excitable cells in your brain. Once you're around tribes that matter to you, the brain sends out a new message: *"Oh, wait. That's not a dingo."*

But what if you can't reach out? What if you get the news when you're at work or away on a trip? Psychologist Guy Winch has some clever advice—get a "social snack." In his book, *Emotional First Aid, Healing Rejection, Guilt, Failure and Other Everyday Hurts,* he points to studies that show how purposefully looking at pictures of people you love eases emotional pain.

In one study, subjects were asked to vividly remember a significant rejection while looking at photographs. Half the subjects looked at photos of celebrities they did not know. The other half looked at family and friends they loved. The subjects who looked at pictures of celebrities reported a large mood drop while those who looked at pictures of loved ones did not.

This is a powerful remedy to have in your psychological medicine cabinet. Put photographs of people you care about on your desk or somewhere in your line of sight. If that's not possible create a "Rejection Relief" photo album on your smartphone filled with friends and family that you feel strongly connected to. The next time you receive a rejection pull it out, look at the pictures and you will blunt the sting far faster than if you tried to think positively or talk yourself out of feeling bad.

If you want to see a movie that accurately portrays the power of "social snacking" Winch suggests you see Tom Hanks in *Cast Away*. Hanks' character is literally cast away from all tribes. How does he cope with social isolation? By looking at a photograph of his girlfriend and talking out loud to a volleyball he named "Wilson." Both helped him feel connected to his tribes.

Photographs are not the only thing you can "snack" on. Studies show that simply recalling positive events (a wedding, a laughing jag) and the people in them can reduce emotional pain. So can reading meaningful emails or letters or watching videos of loved ones or even holding a valued memento.

"Feasting" on your social connections (having a beer with a group, going to lunch with a treasured friend) is better than "snacking"—the sense of connection is stronger—but you don't have to choose. Why not do both?

"Remaining in the tribe" is a powerful human need and this explains much of the appeal for Alcoholics Anonymous. It is the one tribe that will not cast you out no matter how much you misbehave. Your spouse may leave you, your employee may fire you, your parents may kick you out but you are always welcome at AA. It is a tribe that will never abandon you.

Making The Positive Stick Like Velcro

The brain's neural soil is more habitable for weeds than flowers.

Negative events, reactions and memories grow like Kudzu because the brain plants it in pH-balanced soil, fertilizes it with home-grown manure and soaks it with artesian water. Unfortunately, it leaves positivity on the surface, unplanted, unwatered and vulnerable to winds that blow it into the ether.

That is simply the way things are. But they are not the way they have to stay. We may be stuck with the brain's built-in negative bias but we are NOT stuck with the brain's treatment of the positive as ephemeral, ethereal and impermanent.

Neuroscientists believe we can change and grow our neural pathways to receive, store and retrieve positive events as robustly as we do negative ones if we use *conscious* thoughts and actions.

The first thing we need to understand is that we *consciously* ignore or minimize positive or good facts in our lives. For example, you might ignore your child's delightful laugh while writing an important email to your editor. But if that child were to scream and cry you'd stop what you're doing and go over to her. We ALWAYS pay more attention to the bad than the good. It's not that we don't notice the positive; it's that we don't act as strongly toward pleasure the way we act toward pain. The good news is that this is a conscious choice that can be reversed.

Second, even when we do notice and experience a positive we don't dwell on it very long. Get a great review? You'll speed-read through it once and put it away. A bad one? You'll read it word-for-word, return to it repeatedly and complain to your friends about it. Again, we don't choose our reactions but we choose the actions that follow it. In other words, you don't have a choice about a brain highjacked by alarm, but you DO have a choice about emailing the bad review to your friends and adding more pitch and volume to that alarm.

Third, we tend to minimize, deflect, and even deride positive events. What was your reaction the last time somebody paid you a compliment? "Oh, this old thing! I got it a thrift shop!" "Thanks, I like that chapter too but the rest of it sucks." Somebody says you look particularly good today and you might grunt in acknowledgement but quickly change the subject.

This phenomenon extends to most positive experiences. Let's say you've agonized over a chapter for weeks and you've finally completed it. This is a good thing. A GREAT thing, but instead of absorbing the positive experience, celebrating it, calling your tribe, you move on to the next chapter, because hey, who has time to celebrate when the dingo's at your door?

And even when you actually do acknowledge a positive event (your agent actually called you back in a timely manner for once!) you typically don't stay with the experience long enough for it to shape your neural structure or store it in long-term memory like you do for negative events (unless it's a life-changing event like Penguin and Simon & Schuster bidding on your book).

The net effect of ignoring, minimizing or even denying something good in our lives is that the positive ends up exactly where our brains greeted it—on top of unfertilized dirt and vulnerable to the wind blowing it off the topsoil. Let's summarize this phenomenon:

How We Treat The Negative	How We Treat The Positive
• We scan for it	• We overlook it
• Maximize it	• Minimize it
• React with high intensity	• React with low intensity
• Embrace it	• Deflect
• Tune in	• Tune out
• Over-react	• Under-react
• Remember it for a long time	• Quickly forget it
• Consider it a personal attack	• Brush it off as luck

This is where neuroscientists like Rick Hanson believe we have the chance to make profoundly beneficial changes to our brains— to groove them with neural patterns that make the positive stick like Velcro instead of Teflon.

"Neurons That Fire Together Wire Together"

This clever phrase was first used in 1949 by Donald Hebb, a Canadian neuropsychologist known for his work in associative learning. Hebb's axiom says every experience, thought, feeling, and physical sensation triggers thousands of neurons, which form a neural network. Your brain is EXPERT at making neural networks out of the negative. It is not nearly as good doing it with the positive.

Time to give fate a little nudge.

Our job is to get neurons firing about positive facts so they'll wire up positive neural structures. Over time this will lower the intensity of the brain's built-in negativity bias and allow us to come from love not fear, calm not anxiety and strength not weakness.

How To Create Positive Neural Networks

We are going to make the brain's soil as welcoming to flowers as it is to weeds and we're going to do it by consciously mimicking the strategies your built-in negative bias uses.

Step 1: Scan For The Positive

Your built-in negative bias stands sentry 24/7 looking for danger. It's on automatic; not something you're even aware of. While scanning for the positive is a weak feature of the brain, it is something we can strengthen with our conscious mind. Here's how:

Notice Your Foreground And Background.
Positive people, events, feelings and circumstances are all around us but we often don't notice them because they're small and don't capture our attention. We don't have to scan for the big things, like a starred review from Publishers Weekly, because it finds us. But we have to scan for the little things like a Google Books review because they escape us. Your job is to look for gestures, quiet pleasures, the bits and bobs of bliss that make up every day life. They include:

People

How does your editor or agent make you feel when you've had a productive conversation? Did a writer friend compliment your manuscript? Do you feel close to your child or partner right now? What about the stranger who kindly allowed you to take the parking space she was waiting for?

Emotional States

Do you feel hopeful after hanging up with your agent? Are you feeling cozy because the cat's curled up by your laptop as you write? Are you calm? Happy? Joyful? Are you feeling particularly close to a friend, your partner, an associate, a child? Do you feel proud of the presentation in front of the boss?

Accomplishments

Did you get all the letters out to publishers? Did you win the tennis game? Complete a task? Contacted bloggers to get reviews?

Physical pleasure

Are you sitting in a comfortable chair? Did you catch a whiff of home-made chocolate (CHOCOLATE!) cookies? What did it feel like to take your shoes off at the end of the day? Did you have a particularly good love-making session?

Events

Did you go to a writing seminar and learn something helpful? Did you go to the stadium and see your favorite team win?

<u>Beauty</u>
Did you finish a book that put you in a state of grace? Did you spot a beautiful oak tree? Are you sitting in the lobby of a hotel with a beautiful painting? Do you like the sturdiness of your wooden dinner table?

Step 2: Create The Positive

If you can't find it, make it. Play some music, go for a walk, call a friend, go to a play, do something that will create genuine pleasure.

Step 3: Absorb And Celebrate The Positive NOW Not Later

Typically, we wait to "count our blessings" right before going to bed or upon waking. Or we give thanks at the beginning of a meal. Gratefulness is helpful but not what we're going for. Our goal is to experience the positive *as it happens*, not recollect it later so we can be grateful for it. Neural networks build faster and last longer when we experience affirmative emotions and maximize their intensity *in the moment*.

Step 4: Stay The Hell Away From Positive Thinking.

Your brain knows when you're trying to put lipstick on a pig. Don't take a negative and try to make a positive out of it. Don't spin it or try to see the good in the bad or find the silver lining in the cloud. Neural networks don't get built when you step in shit and look for a pony. They get built when you step in shit, win $300 and replace the shit-laced shoes with a pair of Loboutins. Scan, find and absorb *genuinely* positive events in your life.

Step 5: Celebrate The Positive The Way You Panic At The Negative

Here's what typically happens when you get a bad review: You flood with negative images and feelings. Anger mixes with outrage, shame and humiliation. You heighten the intensity by complaining to friends, agents, and writing compatriots. You go on a "what-iffing" binge. What if this is the beginning of many more bad reviews to come? Is this the end of your career? What if your editor sees this? Is she going to look down on you? You email the review to family or friends with a "Can you believe this Jackass" note. You feel unmasked. Maybe the reviewer is right—you're a poser, a fake. You blog about it.

Here's what typically happens when you get a good review: You smile and move on.

This is why negatives neural networks grow like easy-to-spread Kudzu and positive ones like hard-to-grow orchids. The challenge before us is to treat the positive with the intensity we treat the negative. We don't just let the negative wash over us. We pick it apart. We dwell on it. We analyze it. We imagine their consequences. So let's do that with the positive:

Old Response To Getting A Good Review: Smile and move on.

New Response To Getting A Good Review: You smile, pump your fist. You re-read it. You read it OUT LOUD. You intensify it by dancing a little jig, clapping and giving yourself a bow. You email it to your friends and have a celebratory drink. You feel vindicated. Maybe the reviewer is right—you have talent that is not being recognized by the public at large! You go on a "what-if" binge. What if this is the start of many more positive reviews? What if bloggers are so moved by it that they pick up the book and review it themselves? What if a slew of great critiques captures the attention of a high-powered agent? You imagine great and wonderful consequences.

This is how you build positive neural networks—the same way you build negative ones. You scan for, find, heighten, maximize and absorb positive developments. You stay with the feeling longer than you usually do. You intensify it in any way you can. You burst out saying, "This is Spectacula like Dracula!" You find something fresh or novel about it. You help it nourish you and make a difference in your life. *You absorb it.*

Do not EVER smile at a positive occurrence and move on. All you'll do is leave the positivity laying on the surface of the topsoil where all those damn squirrels can steal them.

Plant those positives deep in the soil. Fertilize them. Water them.

Step 6: Spend The Proper Amount Of Time "Installing" Positive Experiences

On a day to day basis most affirmative moments are small and fairly inconsequential. Treat them that way. Doing somersaults and breaking out the champagne may be an appropriate response to watching your book land on the best seller list, but not when you simply get an unexpected compliment. In those small moments (and there are a lot more of them than big moments) simply take the time to notice them and let yourself feel good about it. You don't need to announce it to the world but you do need to spend about 30 seconds reveling in it (that's about the time it takes for your neurons to fire and wire around an experience). Let the good experience sink into you. Take half a minute to visualize how you're absorbing the experience. Personally, I picture the seed of the experience being planted in fertile soil and watching a sprinkler water it.

Doing this once is inconsequential. Doing it twice only slightly more so. But doing it five or six times a day over the course of a few of months—that's when you activate the law of little things, best summed up in the phrase, "Take care of the minutes and you'll take care of the years."

Making The Temporary Permanent

By changing the way you recognize and react to positive experiences you help as Rick Hanson says, "turn a passing mental state into a lasting neural structure."

The brain is a physical system that encompasses mechanical, chemical and electrical processes. It is highly adaptive. Like a muscle it gets stronger the more you use it. "Brain Change" is a process in which an activated experience (positive or negative) gets installed in long-term memory by creating a neural network. As Hanson states:

> "Without installation, there is no learning, no change: in effect, the experience is wasted on the brain. This is the dirty little secret in most psychotherapy, human resources training, coaching, addiction recovery, and character education: most hard-won beneficial states of mind—including experiences of grit—are momentarily positive but have no lasting value."

This is a crucial aspect of developing a bulletproof conscience —"installing" positive experiences in the brain for lasting value. Good experiences of determination, endurance, resolve and perseverance can be largely ineffective if you don't encode them into the brain with deliberate mindful attention, sustaining them and intentionally absorbing their benefits. Without that encoding you can "survive" a truly harrowing experience (like having the negotiations over a six figure advance suddenly collapse) without extracting long-term benefits, leaving you just as vulnerable to future stress, loss or setbacks.

Slowing The Neural Onslaught

Once you understand how your brain gets "highjacked by alarm" you can gain more control of the ancient circuitry and self-sooth in effective ways. Always start by opening a cognitive umbrella during a neural storm. As in, "Ah, my brain is reacting with a threat response. It thinks that the rejection I got means the tribe is kicking me out and the dingo's coming for my baby."

Once you've emotionally connected to other tribes in your life—through in-person contact, phone calls or looking at photographs —you'll notice a dramatic and significant change in your emotional state. This means you've essentially shut off the false alarm, but it doesn't mean you've completely solved the problem. We've confirmed it's not a dingo.

So what is it?

Chapter Five

Emotional First Aid:
Managing The Pain Of Rejection

We now have an intellectual understanding of what is happening to us. Rejection stresses us because our brain's ancient circuitry flashes, "Dingo! Dingo! Dingo!" So far, we've clearly proven that it's not a wild dog coming for your baby, so what is it?

A door. A shut door. A door that is not going to open again. That is all it is and it is all that. A shut door isn't a dingo but it can still bring up powerful emotions that you must deal with. The bulletproof consciousness doesn't simply keep calm and carry on. It deals with emotional pain in a responsible way to process, heal and move forward.

Feel Your Pain And Then Feel It Some More.
Feelings are like tax collectors—they won't go away no matter how long you ignore them. Eventually, they're going to catch up with you. You can pay now when the taxes are low (a crying jag or two, a few heart-to-heart conversations, a couple of rounds on the punching bag) or later when the interest outstrips the original bill (depression, anxiety, paralysis, wretched writing).

The more you deny or bury your feelings, the more they tend to manifest in undesirable ways. Feelings were meant to be felt.

Refusing to cry or express the anger, futility, pity or hopelessness you feel will mess you up far worse than the temporary discomfort of dealing with it as it happens.

Many writers try to control their emotions by trying to change the rejection itself. For example, Mrs. Writer gets a bad review. Outraged and hurt, she contacts the reviewer and reads him the riot act. Mr. Author, upon receiving a rejection of his new manuscript by a publisher who made a lot of money off his last few books, gets on the phone and tries to guilt the editor into accepting it.

This is what's known as "stacking" emotional pain. You incur a hurt and then stack it with more emotional turmoil. Now you have to deal with the original hurt as well as the disaster you created by your unwillingness to accept the inevitable.

The Goal Isn't To Feel Better

The goal of expressing your feelings isn't to make you feel better about a loss. Why would you want to feel good about a rejected manuscript? Or having an agent tell you he no longer wants to represent you? These are not things you should feel better about. The goal isn't to feel good about something awful but to center yourself, to put yourself in a better frame of mind to move forward. It is to lift the veil that emotions place over your eyes so you can see the all-encompassing truth about rejection: *It is a short chapter in a much larger book.*

You don't have to feel good about the chapter. You just have to be strong enough to turn the page.

The 48 Hour Sulking Rule

"Feeling your feelings" doesn't come without risks. It's entirely possible to descend into an emotional quicksand and stay there. It is a legitimate fear with plenty of evidence to back it up. Ever met anybody who let themselves get angry and then stayed angry for years? Fortunately there are ways to process your feelings without drowning in them. Mark Mcguinness, in his book, *Resilience: Facing Down Rejection And Criticism On The Road To Success* talks about soccer manager Martin O'Neill's brilliant approach to avoiding this trap: The 48 hour Sulking Rule. If his team lost, O'Neill allowed his players a two-day grieving period. For 48 hours, they could scream, cry, throw fits, sulk and play the blame game. But afterwards? It was "GAME OVER" on the last game. He expected his team, having stewed, processed, and expressed their discontent and grief to get back to the task at hand.

O'Neill essentially put term limits on his team's emotions. He knew first-hand the folly of putting a manhole cover over powerful feelings. Interestingly, he instituted the 48 Hour Rule for victory, too. Every time his team won they were allowed 48 hours to celebrate and then it was back to work and no mention of the previous win.

O'Neill understood that unfelt feelings created as many problems as unending feelings. Imagine if his soccer team continued to celebrate—or grieve—past the 48-hour mark. Discipline would collapse, the focus would blur and the will to win would recede.

Applying The 48 Hour Sulking Rule To Writing

Jeffrey Davis is the author of *The Journey from the Center to the Page: Yoga Philosophies and Practices as Muse for Authentic Writing*. He's so good at the 48 Hour Sulking Rule he wrote this amusing little anecdote in *Psychology Today*:

> "When I got the first editorial letter back from my editor at Penguin for the first edition of The Journey From the Center to the Page, the manuscript came back and I got an eleven-page, single-spaced letter, and I think there were maybe four sentences that were positive that said, "I think you have a lot of good ideas," and the rest was the details of everything that needed to change. And I could see her red pencil that just made these big loops on page after page so I literally went to bed for forty-eight hours.
>
> My wife peeked her head in and she said, "Are you ok?" I said, "I will be in forty-eight hours."

Davis gave himself two days to cry, sulk, and spiral into a depression. He entered his wine and chocolate phase, set up the shame fest and jumped into the Humiliation Hole. He did it because he knew it was necessary for him to get to a place where he could see the editor's rejection for what it was—a temporary setback.

Clearly, you don't need a 48 hour sulking rule for every rejection that comes your way. Getting a form rejection letter from a small

Anger As A Tonic

Depression, despair and anxiety aren't the only emotions to process. What about anger? Here's what novelist and screenwriting raconteur Chuck "I am likely drunk and untrustworthy" Wendig has to say:

"Build a wall. A shrine. A goddamn *memorial* display of all your rejections. Writers need to gain emotional power over their rejections. By embracing them and putting them up for all to see, you claim that power. Show it to others. Laugh at it. Find ways to surpass it. Stephen King reportedly collected all of his on a nail. I might stuff mine in a giant wicker man. When I die, I will be burned alive inside the rejectionist's pyre."

publisher you've never heard of will not register the kind of pain that having a publisher withdraw their six-figure offer will.

There's nothing magical about "48 Hours." The magic is in the twin goals of allowing yourself to feel bad without getting trapped in your feelings. Some rejections may only take a few minutes to process, some a few hours and others—the kind that make you pronounce all four e's in "shit"—take a few days or more. Typically, the larger the stakes, the sharper the pain and thus, the longer the sulk. For example, a few years ago talk show icon Katie Couric was captivated by my book, *Not Tonight Dear, I Feel Fat: How To Stop Worrying About Your Body & Have Great Sex.*

Couric and her producers wanted to do an entire segment of her show around the book. They bought 100 copies to give out to the live studio audience and they booked my ticket to New York City for the taping. I spent hours on the phone with the producers answering questions and prepping for the interview.

You can imagine my excitement. The savannah was about to welcome its newest white rhino! Champagne and cocaine here I come! There was no doubt that kind of publicity would explode the book into the best seller lists. Then I got a phone call *the night before the taping*. They had changed their minds. No New York. No Champagne. No Cocaine.

I was in so much shock I had to stick my finger up my ass and yell "snake" to get my dick to pop out.

Seriously, I want to tell you something: I only cry in movies. That night, I cried. To this day I can't think back to the memory of the phone call without my chest tightening. One could argue that kind of rejection warranted a 48-DAY sulking rule. I hardly worked from the stress and disappointment and called everyone that could help me process it. I knew that I had to put term limits on my grief but I also knew this wasn't a regular rejection. So I allowed myself more than 48 hours. In fact, if I had stayed in my bedroom for much longer they would have put my face on a milk carton. But afterwards, I literally said to myself, "I will never speak of this again." And I haven't, until now.

Form A Mental Blockade To Keep Out Solutions

The 48-hour sulking period should have a sign on it: SOLU-

TIONS AREN'T WELCOME. This is a period of grieving, raging at God and kicking dirt. You are here to process feelings not entertain solutions or forge a path forward. There will be plenty of time for that later. There is a process to healing. Rushing in with well-meaning advice is counter-productive. It's like having a pet die and having a friend ask if you're going to get another one. Hello? Can I just have a moment to myself to sort out the past and present before I address the future? There is an order to the universe. Night follows morning. Spring follows winter. Planning follows sorrow.

The Post 48-Hour Sulking Period

The tears stop, the rage subsides, the scab forms. Now what? For most of us, the worst is over emotionally, but we're not quite where we should be because what we went through probably wasn't our first, third or tenth rejection. It's probably Rejection Number Insert Your Score Here. And that means we've created a story around the rejection, a narrative we can't get out of our heads: "This is the end of the road, I'm no good, my work is irrelevant, no one wants it, I've failed."

We need some proven strategies to bleach the negative out and keep us empowered. Let's take a look at some of the more ingenious solutions that recent scientific research has provided us.

Whatever You Do, Don't THINK POSITIVELY.

I mentioned earlier that optimism is a great disposition to have but a lousy strategy to use. There is lots of evidence that using positive thinking as a way of moving past emotional pain can actually make things worse.

For example, the typical positive thinking approach is to argue against a negative judgment. So if you are feeling worthless because you got rejected, the typical advice is to look yourself in the mirror and say, "I'm worthwhile" dozens of times and then to journal how worthwhile you are and write it down a hundred times. It's all about advancing a positive counter-argument to the monkey chatter in your brain. Think you're a terrible writer? Then write about all those great Amazon reviews.

As anyone who has attempted this kind of positive thinking approach knows, it rarely works. Remember our built-in negativity bias? Negative thoughts and experiences come more easily, stay longer and are felt far more powerfully than positive thoughts. *The brain welcomes negative with Velcro and positive with Teflon.* Trying to overcome a negative narrative with a positive story line is like using a Tic Tac to fight a whale's bad breath. Or trying to outbox Muhammad Ali—you're going to get a big helping of floor.

A more effective approach would be to borrow from both Buddhism and behaviorism. Instead of trying to convince yourself that you're worthwhile sit yourself down and endlessly repeat the words "I'm worthless."

Wait, WHAT?

Draining The Power Out Of Judgment

Sounds insane but there's a method to the madness. Buddhism calls it a way to transcend the ego. Behaviorism calls it "extinction"—the process of desensitizing yourself to a feared thought or object to the point that it has no power over you. Try it right now. Pick a comfortable chair, close your eyes and repeat whatever obsessive thought you can't get rid of. Let's say it's, "Nobody wants to read my work." Say it loud. See the words in your mind. Do it for several minutes—repeat the words and the image—and an amazing thing will happen. At first, you'll agree with yourself vehemently. You might feel the emotion so powerfully you'll cry. All kinds of negative images and feelings will flash by but keep repeating the words and holding them as an image in your mind. Slowly, *ever so slowly*, the constant repetition desensitizes you. The color drains out. Emotion and judgment disappear, leaving you with repeating words that are empty of meaning.

There is a great tradition in Buddhism of repeating negative thoughts over and over and over again because eventually they stop triggering *any* meaning (negative or positive) and essentially become nothing but sound. It is at that point that you can see a more divine truth—the words you're repeating simply make up a story that doesn't reflect objective reality.

And once you've achieved that kind of equilibrium you realize that good/bad, worthwhile/worthless are words the ego uses to judge itself and others. But you are way more than your ego, and as you float past it in your mind, you think about your mission: To gift the "powerful play" with your own verse. And now the possibility exists not to construct a negative or positive view of yourself, but to stoke the burning desire of contributing your verse.

Observe & Accept

There's another surprising way to combat the negative view of yourself that endless rejections can dredge up. Once again, you need to forget about "positive thinking" as a solution. Remember what brain science researcher Rick Hansen said: *"Negative contaminates positive more than positive purifies negative."* Meaning, fighting negativity with positivity is like using a toothpick to fight a guy with a sword.

So how do you fight against negativity without positivity? Through a Buddhist tradition I call "Watching The Weather." Lay down and close your eyes for a few minutes. Picture a cloudless blue sky. Now picture a rejected manuscript, a bad review or poor sales as a series of clouds that increasingly block your view of the blue sky. Let the clouds do whatever they want to do—turn gray, black, storm, thunder, hail, whatever. Sometimes my clouds point at me, turn into Truman Capote and screech in that high pitch voice of his, "That's not writing, that's *typing!*" Other times my clouds turn into hideous villains that say things like "I've read your writing. I'VE STEPPED IN DEEPER PUDDLES!"

Don't respond to whatever you see in the sky. Don't judge it—just observe. Don't try to lighten the clouds if they're dark, or disperse them if they've accumulated. Don't argue with them if they attack. Just observe. Accept. Don't resist. Eventually, the clouds, accepted and unresisted will exit stage left and you'll be left with a lot more blue sky. Problems are like the weather. Clouds form, they darken, they empty their stores and when they're done, they move on.

And then they come back, form, darken, empty and move on again. This is the cycle of life (and of problems). There is no such thing as a constant blue sky just as there is no such thing as a rejection-free writer's life. The clouds and the rejections will come and then they'll go.

Enjoy the scenery.

Managing Emotional Pain Like Physical Pain

Psychologists have long studied people in chronic physical pain and they've come up with remarkable solutions that also work on emotional pain. For example, psychologists know that the meaning we give pain dramatically improves our ability to tolerate it.

If you tripped on a curb and hurt your leg, you'd experience a lot more pain if you convinced yourself it was tissue damage rather than a pulled muscle. One study showed that women *experienced* more pain from cancer than childbirth, even though pain level intensities are the same. Why? Because getting cancer is perceived as a much worse condition than giving birth.

What's the connection to emotional pain? Let's take a divorce as an example. Which would hurt more—if you divorced your partner because he was having an affair or because he's an alcoholic? The blame you assign determines the level of pain you experience.

How This Applies To Writers

Your manuscript got rejected. Is it because you're a lousy writer or because the manuscript wasn't right for that publisher? Is it because your story had the depth of a sophomore term paper or because the publishing house has three similar books coming out in the spring? Shift the "why" of your rejection and you shift the level of the pain.

Your belief in the source of the pain alters your experience of it.

Studies also show that *where* you put your concentration can significantly decrease pain. In one study, women in labor who focused on the pain itself reported double the intensity than women who focused on the beautiful baby they were birthing.

Here too, writers can take advantage of this finding. Writers who focus on the pain of rejections themselves will suffer more than writers who concentrate on the fact that failure is a precursor to success. Remember Dean Simonton's research? *Successful people suffer more failures than unsuccessful people.* Through his research Simonton proved the old adage that every NO gets you closer to a YES; that failure is not a dead-end; it's part of the long swim to success. You will alter the perception of pain if you move your focus from *"I've been rejected"* to I'M GETTING CLOSER.

You Can Because You Have

Yet another way of improving our ability to manage pain is to compare it to past experiences of similar pain. We can remind ourselves that we've survived similar pain before. And if we did it before we can do it again. Studies show that this type of attitude has significant pain-reducing benefits. Some researchers believe that recollections of previous "Pain survivals" may explain why women report their second delivery as less painful than the first, even though from a physical perspective there is no reason it should be. In fact, there's much research that shows the more familiar we are with the pain, the more we've experienced it, the less pain it causes us.

Believing in our ability to handle pain increases our tolerance of it.

Take Two Tylenol And Call Me In The Morning

Although the experience of physical pain is different than emotional pain, functional imaging studies show both types of pain light up the same regions of the brain. So intertwined are the experiences of physical and emotional pain researchers recently made a startling discovery: Tylenol can relieve the pain of hurt feelings.

Baldwin Way, a psychologist at Ohio State University and the principal investigator on the study told NPR: "It seems to take the highs off your daily highs and the lows off your daily lows. It kind of flattens out the vicissitudes of your life."

Yes, the medicine you take for a headache works for a heartache. Acetaminophen dulls the effects of negative emotions. Remember our ball tossing experiment? Subjects who were given two Tylenol reported less emotional pain after being excluded from the ball toss than the subjects who didn't take it! Consider taking Tylenol if you've hit a particularly rough patch.

Future-Proof Yourself

Think about losses you thought you'd never get over—a lover, a job, a missed opportunity. Indeed, you healed, got a different job, a better lover and gained more opportunities. What changed? The passage of time revealed an essential truth about the brain's built-in negativity bias—it ensures that we will blow almost every piece of bad news out of proportion. The good news is that we have a long history of getting past that initial blow and rising above it.

What would the present you tell the old you about never dating again after someone broke your heart? What would the current you tell the former you about that job you didn't get? Most likely that things got better and in many cases a whole lot better than the old you could have imagined.

You can use this exercise to address the current rejections you're facing. What would the you of a couple of years from now tell the present you? That you were right for freaking out, beating yourself up and giving up hope? Or that you will arrive at a place of wisdom, love and calm?

Sometimes the only way to gain perspective of your current situation is to remember how badly you thought other things were in your past and compare them to the present. You will come to the realization that you're a lot more resilient than you give yourself credit for. Rejections may feel bad today but they'll seem insignificant in a few years or even a few weeks. Picture yourself a few months from now looking back at the rejection you have today. What do you see? What do you feel? I promise it will not be what you see and feel right now.

Suzy Welch, in her book, *10-10-10: A Life-Transforming Idea* has a simple premise. Upon a difficult decision she applies a 10-10-10 formula by asking herself three questions:

1. What are the consequences of my decision in 10 minutes?
2. In 10 months?
3. In 10 years?

We can use her formula to get perspective on a rejection. What will we feel 10 minutes from now? Horribly, no doubt. In 10 months? We'll remember it as a negative but without much emotional charge. In 10 years? We might actually see it for what it was—bad luck, a temporary setback, and quite possibly, a necessary—though painful—step to arriving where you are now.

You Don't Have To Stop Feeling Bad To Start Feeling Good.

For highly complicated beings we tend to oversimplify our cognitive abilities. For example, most people think they can't start feeling good until they stop feeling bad. But if you're an astute observer of the human condition you know that we can feel multiple emotions at the same time. In fact, it's fairly rare to only feel one emotion at a time. And often you can have wildly divergent emotions simultaneously. For example, my accident-prone father would often take Chevy Chase-like pratfalls. I could not stop laughing even though I was alarmed about his safety. How could I be entertained AND concerned at the same time? Because I'm human and I'm capable of experiencing multiple— and contradictory—feelings at the same time.

Certainly this is true in writing. I was elated that a publisher bought my third book but depressed by the size of the advance. I was both proud and ashamed all at the same time.

Our emotional moods are not controlled by an on/off switch. They're controlled by a panel of dials, each in some stage of brightness or darkness. It is actually rare to feel one emotion so powerfully that it crowds out all others and even if it does, it doesn't last long.

It only *seems* like we have to feel one emotion before starting another but that's only because events tend to stop or start a single emotion. Our natural ability to hold different emotions is a key to overcoming our negativity bias. Instead of trying to "eliminate" negative thoughts and feelings (ha!) why not compete with them? For example, expressing gratitude for what you have (a publishing deal) doesn't mean denying a painful loss (half the advance you were hoping for); it means holding both realities at the same time.

What If You're Still Stuck After A Reasonable Sulking Period?

Nobody is saying you'll be healed in 48 hours or whatever term limit you've set for yourself. Remember, the point isn't to feel better about something awful; it's to center yourself for the next step. Deep, gutting, major rejections like my talk show debacle aside, if you can't get most of your emotions out in a reasonable time frame, you have to face that you're not trying to "process" anything; you've fallen victim to a mental process psychologists call "Rumination"—a vicious circle of repeated thoughts, replayed scenes, relived trauma and play-by-play recollections.

You know you've slipped into rumination when the thinking feels compulsive and never ends with an emotional release, a comforting insight or any sense of relief. Instead, it leads to an intensification of the emotional psychological distress you already feel.

Fortunately, psychologists have recently discovered two novel solutions that are far more effective than even talk therapy. Cheaper, too. Let's take a look.

Chapter Six

Ruminations: Dealing With Rejections You Can't Seem To Get Over

When we get a painful rejection it's normal to process our feelings, reflect on what happened, sort things out and gain some perspective. But under particularly painful rejections, a genuine attempt at self-soothing and self-reflection can lead to rumination —repeated thoughts that perpetuate our distress. We replay the same scenes over and over again without coming to any new understanding. What starts out as a need for clarification and release ends up trapping us in emotional loops where we endlessly replay the same distressing feelings.

How Do You Know When You're In The Throes Of Rumination?

With self-reflection you go through a short, turbulent period and slowly, insights arrive. Feelings subside. Acceptance flickers. Calm sets in. Memories of the rejection may still be painful but they don't carry the electric charge they once did. There is a sense of carrying forward.

This stage lasts anywhere from a few hours to a couple of days (48 Hour Sulking Rule) but depending on the depth of the rejection can last longer. You know you've slipped into rumination when you're constantly thinking about the rejection but the thoughts illuminate nothing. No new insights arrive. No new epiphanies. You slip further away from balance and centeredness and in fact, you're not lowering the intensity through "processing" you are increasing it with obsessive thoughts.

Psychologists often think of rumination as "Anger inflation"—a way of fanning the flames of sadness, rage, hurt and alienation. If self-reflection throws water at the fire, rumination throws lighter fluid. It intensifies sadness and anger and makes them persist longer. It involves intense brooding that consumes huge amounts of mental energy—energy that can be stored for writing. It impairs our concentration, our motivation, our initiative and our problem-solving abilities. It takes up a substantial amount of intellectual and emotional resources. It also has the ability to affect relationships because, come on, how long can your friends and family listen to the awfulness that has befallen you?

Rumination is a particularly difficult hamster wheel to step out of because of its self-reinforcing nature. Ruminating about a rejection make you more upset. The more upset you are the more you want to think about the problem because you think you have to process your feelings.

How "Talking It Out" Increases Rumination

Ruminations form urgent needs to talk through your feelings. What could be wrong with that? A lot, it turns out. Once you get past a reasonable "statute of limitations" (24-72 hours for most rejections), research studies show that expressing your feelings through talk is counter-productive.

Even traditional talk therapies have had limited success in stopping rumination. For instance, talk therapies that ask patients to recount their problems in great detail tend to increase ruminating tendencies. Even cognitive behavioral therapy, which places much less emphasis on feelings, can inadvertently cause more rumination. When you are asked to identify negative thoughts so you can dispute them you are in essence teaching people how to ruminate.

Suppressing Thoughts & Feelings Makes Things Worse

Trying to stop rumination through will power is like, Garth Brooks wrote in his song "The Change," "Trying to stop a fire with the moisture of a kiss." Studies show that the attempt to suppress thoughts ends up amplifying them instead. In the classic "Don't think of a white bear" experiments subjects were told not to think of a white bear for five minutes and to ring the bell every time they failed. You can imagine how many times that bell rang. Not only did the subjects fail spectacularly, many experienced a rebound effect in which they could not stop thinking about white bears even after the experiment was over.

Will power, or thought suppression is a complete waste of time.

Scientists have lately made new discoveries about the best approaches to stop rumination and they do not involve talking. The first step is to cut off rumination's fuel source: The intensity of your emotions. It is the strength of your feelings that give rise to the repeated thoughts. Weaken the feelings and you weaken the urge to ruminate. Makes sense. The less upset you feel, the less thoughts you're going to have about the upset. So how do you weaken the negative feelings?

It Works For Toddlers; It'll Work For You

Think of rumination as the brain's version of a toddler's tantrum. How do you stop a wiggly two-year-old's upset? Distraction. Look! Shiny keys! Shake, shake, shake! You don't even need an object. Sometimes it can be a simple question. In a wildly popular YouTube video you can see a father completely distracting his two-year-old's melt-down with a simple question: "What's a cow say?" The child stops crying and says, "moo." In another scene he asks, "Where's your tongue?" The child stops crying and sticks her tongue out. Then the father sticks his tongue out and they both start laughing.

Dealing with rumination is a little like dealing with a toddler. Neither responds to logic or reason. You cannot sit either of them down and explain the need for more appropriate behavior. The only way to stop the emotional trajectory is to give the emotions another path to follow. Now, clearly you are not going to distract your rumination by shaking shiny keys in front of your eyes or asking yourself what a cow says. Before we talk about effective distraction techniques, let's explore the concept a little further.

Tempting Your Way Out Of Temptation

Think of rumination as a temptation, an urge to do something that is not good for you. Noted psychologist Walter Mischel's breakthrough studies on resisting temptation offers a clever, dramatically effective approach. Don't resist it; compete with it.

In his studies, he offered small children a choice between having a marshmallow now or having two if they waited fifteen minutes. Imagine 8-year-olds staring at a marshmallow alone in a room for fifteen minutes! Most succumbed. The children most likely to wait out the 15 minutes? The ones coached to picture the pleasure of eating pretzels instead. In other words, imagining the pleasure they'd get from an unavailable temptation (the pretzels) helped them manage the available temptation (marshmallows).

What's The Application For Writers?

It's about using distractions to veer yourself away from thinking or talking about a painful rejection. What kind of distractions? Anything that ordinarily lights you up like an all-night liquor store. Researchers found the most effective distractions have some common elements:

They Arouse Intellectual Curiosity

Playing solitaire might be a distraction but are you really as interested in that as much as a crossword puzzle? Or Sudoku? Surfing the web is distracting but are you searching for things that you're truly curious about or are you landing haphazardly on random sites? The point is to connect with what you are truly curious about. You can't lose yourself in something that mildly interests you. Go for distractions that have a big pull on you.

They Arouse Powerful Emotions

Your goal is to raise your adrenaline level so it distracts and overpowers your rumination. For some that might mean jumping out of an airplane, but it doesn't have to be that dramatic (though it helps). Riding a roller coaster could do it. But then, so could a great horror movie. Don't worry about choosing the right distraction—it doesn't necessarily have to raise your adrenaline, just your attention. If you like to cook, baking home made cookies might do it. If you're going to divert your attention by watching TV, don't watch old reruns of I Love Lucy; watch the latest blockbuster movie you've been dying to see. Don't take a walk around the neighborhood you know like the back of your hand. Drive to a beautiful park you've always wanted to visit and poke around. If you're going to get together with people make sure they're good friends not acquaintances.

They Are Highly Pleasurable

Deep tissue massages are distracting but are they pleasurable or painful? Your choice of distractions should have a high pleasure factor. Don't jog if you feel ambivalent about running; play tennis if you feel more drawn to it. The point is to attend to your pleasure. The more pleasure you experience the more displeasure (rumination) you displace.

Work absolutely qualifies as a distraction—unless it isn't pleasurable, doesn't arouse your curiosity or engage you emotionally. If it does, have at it. If parts of it do, spend more time on those parts.

Of course it's not always possible to take a few hours off to distract ourselves but again the concept of "social snacking" is always available. Take brief breaks to do things you enjoy, like a Sudoku puzzle, or put your ear buds on and listen to a couple of your favorite songs while taking a short walk. Distraction is a proven mood lifter that restores the quality of our thinking and our problem solving abilities.

The Two Week Silence Rule

Using distraction as a technique to relieve rumination won't work if at the end of the distraction you start talking about the rejection you're ruminating over. All you've done is delay the rumination. You have to pair the distraction with silence on the matter. Let's not be naïve, of course you will ruminate after a distraction (at least at first) but that doesn't mean you have to verbalize it. Remember the 48 Hour Sulking Rule? Rumination needs a Two Week Silence Rule. That means once you've launched Operation Distraction you are not allowed to verbalize any aspect of your ruminations. Rumination is not a choice but verbalizing it is. This is where will power really does work. Every time you start talking about the problem stop yourself in mid-sentence, change the subject and find a way to distract yourself.

Silence will strengthen distraction's ability to ease your distress. Talking about your distress, on the other hand, is a way to fling yourself back into rumination's arms.

How Long Can You Keep Distracting Yourself?

It's a fair question. One might ask, "If all I ever do is distract myself how will I ever move forward?" Keep in mind that distraction is not a replacement for "feeling your feelings," processing different emotions, connecting to your tribes, contemplating next steps and generally doing the hard work of self-reflection. It is only a strategy to be employed once you've descended into rumination, where no amount of thinking or talking produces helpful insights or cathartic moments. Besides, distraction is actually one half of the one-two punch leading scientists recommend. The other half is a concept in complete opposition to the immersing effects of rumination. It's called...

Distancing

It's completely natural to analyze a painful experience through your own eyes or what psychologists call a "self-immersed perspective." It's a first-person accounting of the pain. There is no one's perspective but your own. The story unfolds in a narrative form with a vivid play-by-play of what happened. You get in touch with your feelings, you examine them, you let them play out. This is healthy—at first. Self-immersion produces strong benefits if we stay there for a brief amount of time. Once it runs out the clock it often turns to rumination, in which there are no benefits—only more distress.

Fortunately, there is a way of extracting the benefits of self-reflection without the intense pain that accompanies self-immersion. It's called "distancing." If self-immersion requires you to relive events in the first person, self-distancing asks you to do it in third person. In self-immersion you tell your story using the words "Me, I, Mine, Myself and Ours." In distancing you use "He, She, It, Theirs and Themselves." Self-immersion is emotional; self-distancing is intellectual. One is concrete, the other abstract.

Self-immersive thoughts tend to generate a similar level of emotional intensity as the initial distressing event (like, getting a last minute phone call cancelling a talk show appearance!). Self-distancing thoughts, however tend to significantly reduce the intensity of emotions.

In his marshmallow experiments Walter Mischel noticed that children who could delay gratification would often distance themselves from the marshmallow in front of them by turning it into an abstraction. For example, they would imagine it as framed and hanging on the wall. Why? Because, as one child memorably stated, "You can't eat a picture!"

Mischel was so impressed by the power of psychological distancing to resist temptation he went on to study the phenomenon further. He soon discovered new ways to help people "self-distance" from painful experiences like social rejection and heartbreak. In an especially clever study he split people who had experienced overwhelmingly negative feelings from a breakup into two groups. Half were asked to reflect on the breakup from their own perspective and try to understand their feelings (the way we normally process experiences).

But he asked the other half to "visualize the experience from the perspective of a fly on the wall." In other words, to psychologically distance themselves from their own perspectives. The results were dramatic. The self-immersion group that reflected from their individual point of view became more emotional, more agitated and increased their anguish as they relived the breakup. But the self-distanced group showed much fewer emotions, used more abstract terms to describe their feelings and experienced more emotional stability. Mischel proved that seeing things from your own perspective tends to recount and reactivate negative feelings while distancing helps reappraise them.

Later studies corroborated Mischel's discovery—when you process an exceptionally painful rejection from a self-distanced perspective you will experience significantly less emotional pain and repetitive thinking. The act of abstracting your problem allows you to reconstruct your understanding and reinterpret events in ways that lead to new insights and feelings of closure.

Interestingly, results of these later studies didn't just rely on self-reported feelings but on measurable physiological changes. For example, subjects who self-distanced from emotional events like a painful breakup showed a slower rise in blood pressure and a quicker return to normal baseline than people who self-immersed, indicating a lower stress response.

How This Applies To Writers

The point of a self-distanced perspective isn't to deny loss; it's about recounting the story of that loss from a different point of view. It isn't about fudging facts to make yourself feel better; it's about gaining an undiscovered perspective. For it to work you must be authentic and recall events accurately. Let's take the example of speaking at a seminar with other authors. At the end, there are long lines of people waiting to buy your fellow authors' books but only two people in line to buy yours. Ouch! Here are three ways you could process this painful rejection from a self-distanced perspective:

1. The Documentary Film

The narrator (a David Attenborough or James Earl Jones type) describes the rejection you experienced by interviewing everyone involved. He interviews you, the other authors, even the people waiting in line to get their books signed, giving a 360 degree view of what led up to your feelings of rejection.

What To Notice:

If you avoid projecting your thoughts onto the characters in the documentary and imagine answers from their perspective you might be surprised to hear comforting things. For example, one of the authors you served on the panel with might have said, "I was surprised that so few people were in line to buy her book (yours), given how articulate she was during the panel discussion."

Or one of the buyers that didn't buy your book may have told the narrator, "It's not that I didn't like her or didn't find her book interesting, it's that I only had enough money to buy one book."

What To Take Away

Notice the distancing effect the documentary has compared to the immersing effect of recounting the story from only your perspective. The documentary is abstract. It refers to you in the third person not the first. It invites you to see points of view you may have never considered. It provides a more balanced, nuanced view of what happened and helps create a partial or total reframe, leaving you a little bit more empowered.

How To Know You're Doing The Exercise Right

If everyone the narrator interviews shares your perspective then you're watching propaganda, not a documentary. You know you're doing the exercise correctly when you take the time to inhabit each character's point of view to offer a different interpretation than yours.

Imagining a documentary is just one of many distancing strategies. Here are a couple more:

2. *The Authorized Biography*

Let's say you spent $2,000 of your own money to market your book and sold only a handful. Imagine reading a biography about the poor sales in which book marketing experts are asked why they think it happened. Was it because the writing sucked? Or because the marketing was all wrong? Or was it bad timing (ten similar books were released on the same day)? The book contains archival studies, analysis, eyewitness accounts and interviews and gives an honest depiction of all aspects that led to the poor sales.

I once did this for myself after watching the best book I ever wrote fail miserably. At launch, it hit the ground and started digging. So painful. When I did this exercise I remember reading a passage in my imaginary "Authorized Biography" that said, "Michael did everything right. The problem in publishing is that you can do everything right and still fail."

I could never have gotten that insight by simply immersing myself in my own emotions.

3. *The Tourist Attraction*

Imagine only five people show up at a bookstore signing and three of them are your friends. So painful. Recount the event as if it were a tourist attraction and a tour guide (perhaps the bookstore owner) is explaining to the crowd what happened. The tour guide is certified in this particular area of rejection and provides assistance, information and cultural, historical and contemporary interpretations of your loss. This means he or she gives everyone's perspective, not just yours, and gives insights into the historical dimensions and current trends of book events gone wrong.

I did this once and "heard" the tour guide explain to the "tourists" that "The attendance to Michael's book signing was pretty average for somebody who isn't a best seller. Many signings literally have zero people show up."

Again, an insight that I might never have gotten if all I did was immerse myself in my own pain.

4. The Split Screen

Let's say your agent dismisses your latest manuscript and strongly advises you to "write to market" over the phone. Imagine you're watching a split screen so you can see both yourself and the agent. Let the rejection play out. Zoom out further so you can watch the event from a greater distance. Play with the zoom lens so you can get as far away from the conversation as you can while still being able to recount the event.

What was your agent's perspective? You don't have to agree with it but it's helpful to understand it. The point of self-distancing isn't to change your mind, it's to gain perspective.

Distancing Quickies

There are times you simply won't have the luxury of playing out the most effective distancing techniques like the documentary film. You might read a bad review of your book right before an important meeting or get a bad news call from your agent when you're in public. These are the times that call for "distancing quickies"—short but powerful ways of keeping yourself centered and calm upon receipt of unwanted news.

The Letter

Imagine the rejection or the bad news or the painful thought as letters written by people you don't respect. You open them and find they had lots of spelling mistakes, grammatical errors and factual inaccuracies. You can't possibly take this seriously so you rip up the letter and throw it in the garbage.

Thanks For Sharing

Thank your painful thoughts as if they were well-meaning children that handed you a dandelion thinking it was a rose. You're not mad at the children you just think it's nonsensical.

Package Delivery

Imagine the rejection or bad news as a big package that a UPS driver just handed you. It's very heavy and very big. He says you must hold it for a little while and you do. But the longer you hold it the smaller the package becomes and the less it weighs. You do that for a few minutes until the package is so small you simply flick it from your palm.

The 1-2-3 Combo

Distancing and distraction techniques are highly effective tools for bypassing the brain's built-in negativity bias, relieving rumination and providing new perspectives that can leave you calmer and more empowered. Don't choose between them; use both. Start by distracting yourself and when the rumination returns (as it will for a while), use the distancing techniques outlined above. It's a 3-step process:

1. Distract Yourself

Engage in highly pleasurable activities that generate genuine curiosity and arouse positive emotions.

2. Silence Yourself

Do not talk to anyone about the rejection you're trying to get over for a full two weeks.

3. Distance Yourself

Use techniques like the documentary film to move away from emotional immersion toward self-distanced, abstract observations.

These are powerful ways to self-soothe and leave you stronger for the push ahead. They will build resiliency and grit so that you can contribute your verse in more effective ways. Now what happens if you bounce back from all your rejections and sell your first, second or eighth manuscript only to get a string of one and two stars on Amazon?

Let's take a look at the most effective ways of handling critics, criticism and bad reviews.

Chapter Seven

How To Handle Critics,
Criticism, and Bad Reviews

Getting a bad review feels like a stranger looked into your child's eyes and declared it the ugliest baby he's ever seen. It can leave you stunned, speechless and PISSED OFF.

I have seen writers practically cry when they get a bad review, even if it's an outlier compared to all the other stellar reviews they've received. Are they just too emotionally delicate to handle a stranger's opinion or is there something else going on?

Flash back to the two researchers tossing the ball to you, making you feel part of their tribe. Suddenly they stop tossing it to you and your emotions plummet—*even after you're told they were members of the heinous Ku Klux Klan.*

Whether it's a white supremacist's ball toss or a stranger's book review, we are wired to care what the tribe thinks of us. If the reviewer is a literary book critic he's part of the Publishing Tribe that you're trying to stay in or get into—a tribe that provides life-sustaining resources. If the reviewer is an ordinary book buyer, she's part of a tribe called "My Readers"—a tribe that can help you survive by selling more books and influence the Publishing Tribe's view of you.

If even one member of these tribes hates your work the brain automatically flashes DINGO! DINGO! DINGO! It has been programmed for eons to be hypersensitive to your standing in the tribe, lest you and your baby get thrown to the dogs.

Your Stone Age brain doesn't look at the totality of all your reviews. It doesn't care that 99 out of 100 reviews are good because its built-in negative bias is programmed to scan for threats not victories. It treats the positive with passing interest because it means you're safe. It treats the negative with intense alarm because it perceives a threat. This is why logical entreaties to weigh the lopsided differences between 99 good reviews and one bad one can fall short. As Hanson stated, "*Negative contaminates positive more than positive purifies negative.*"

The first and most important thing you can do upon seeing a bad review is to connect to your personal tribes—family, friends, and associates you care about. You're not consciously aware of it but your brain is fearing—or feeling—separation. What's the answer to disconnection? Connection. Of exclusion? Inclusion. Of being kept apart? Getting together.

Only by connecting to your tribes can you calm the brain enough to let reason and logic have an effect. And on that score, there is plenty of restorative insights that can make you whole again. Let's talk about them.

Know That You're Not Alone

Isaac Asimov, the acclaimed science fiction author once said, "Writers, fall into two groups: Those who bleed copiously and visibly at any bad review, and those who bleed copiously and secretly at any bad review."

In other words, you're upset by bad reviews? Welcome to the club —where all the members are distinguished by the arrows sticking out of their backs. It's comforting to know that everyone else has gotten, is getting or is going to get bad reviews—no exceptions. A friend, upon getting his first said to me, "I guess I'm a real writer now." Exactly. Real Writers Get Bad Reviews.

Gifted Writers Get Beat On, Too

Do this right now: Type your favorite book into the Amazon search engine and count the number of bad reviews it got. Clearly, you are not alone. You are not being singled out. Here's a sampling of the kind of bad reader reviews some of our most beloved writers have gotten:

Reader Review	Book
"This is actually a horribly written boring piece of literature. It took me 2 days just to get past the horrible first chapter because there was nothing going on to keep me reading. And I figured if it is already this slow and boring than I have to stop. Stay away from this disgustingly overrated book and disgustingly bad writer."	*Harry Potter and the Sorcerer's Stone* by J.K. Rowling

"I was bored out of my mind from start to finish. With every turn of the page, I thought it'd get better, thinking surely something interesting had to happen or else people wouldn't be so obsessed with it."	*The Hunger Games* by Suzanne Collins
"Maybe it has a deep meaning that I didn't get, but honestly, no! It's just not worth the read."	*Carrie* by Stephen King
"This collection of books is really, really terrible and boring, and I wouldn't wish the task of reading in on my worst enemy."	*The Lord of the Rings* by J.R.R. Tolkien
"It was one of the most boring and shallow books that I have ever read."	*The Great Gatsby* by F. Scott Fitzgerald
"If I were you, I'd peruse it briefly at your neighborhood library before putting hard-earned money out."	*A Wrinkle In Time* by Madeleine L'Engle
"I find myself saying to myself as I read it 'bla bla bla' as that is what the author seems to be saying."	*Shadow Country* by Peter Matthiessen

Opinions are, by definition, subjective. There is nothing that all of the people agree on all of the time. Because all writers receive them, getting bad reviews can actually feel like you're being inducted into the tribe, not getting cast out of it.

The Book Doesn't Belong To You Anymore

Author TJ Klune was once criticized by a bunch of readers and reviewers accusing him of misogyny because some of his characters used the word vagina as an insult. Asked why he never responded to the accusations, he wrote:

When an author writes a book, puts said book up for sale, and has people buy said book with their money/credit/ whatever, the book no longer belongs to the author. It belongs to the person who bought it, and they are allowed to have whatever opinion they want, even if you think it's the wrong one. There is nothing you can do to change reactions to your words printed on the page. And if you insist on pursuing these opinions, there's nothing that says you can't use legitimate criticism to make your next work better.

This is a great perspective to have. Once your manuscript leaves your desk and gets put on sale it's an object on somebody else's shelf. It's their property now and they can treat it as they want— as a treasured item or as a doorstop.

Elizabeth Gilbert agrees. In *Big Magic* she writes:

"I got letters saying, 'I detest everything about you,' and I got letters saying, 'You have written my Bible.' Imagine if I tried

to create the definition of myself based on any of these reactions. I didn't try. And that's the only reason Eat, Pray, Love didn't throw me off my path as a writer—because of my deep and lifelong conviction that the results of my work don't have much to do with me. I can only be in charge of producing the work itself. That's a hard enough job. I refuse to take on additional jobs, such as trying to police what anybody thinks about my work once it leaves my desk.

I also think it was immature of me to expect that I should be allowed to have a voice of expression, but other people should not. If I am allowed to speak my inner truth, then my critics are allowed to speak their interests as well. Fair's fair. If you dare to create something and put it out there then it may accidentally stir up a response."

Your Goal Should Be To Have A Positive Effect On Some Not All

In his book, *On Writing: A Memoir of the Craft*, Stephen King made this observation:

> "You can't please all of the readers all of the time; you can't please even some of the readers all of the time, but you really ought to try to please at least some of the readers some of the time."

Stephen King's last few books each got between 50 to 500 one-star/two star reviews on Amazon. He knows a little something about people not liking his work, despite his mythical sales and stellar reputation. He is living proof that if you write something compelling enough to be loved, it's probably compelling enough to be hated.

Book publishing expert Bronwyn Hemus has a similar but slightly different take. She believes if we're not annoying anyone then we're not saying anything. "Would Stalin have enjoyed Orwell's *Animal Farm?*" she asks. "Would McCarthy have recommended *The Crucible?*" Her point is well taken. You're doing something wrong if you're pleasing everyone.

Salman Rushdie was on the same track about the pitfalls of trying to please everyone when he said, "*The only thing worse than a bad review from the Ayatollah Khomeini would be a good review from the Ayatollah Khomeini.*"

Bad Reviews Are Not A Death Sentence For Your Book

No one bad review, no matter where it comes from, can break your book. You are not a Manhattan restaurant relying on a New York Times food critic to keep its 5-star rating. Book stores brim with best sellers that have lousy reviews from important gatekeepers. This applies to all books from contemporary fan fiction novels like *50 Shades Of Grey* to the classics like *Wuthering Heights*.

It's possible to have thousands of one-star reviews and sell like hot cakes—as long as you have many more three star+ reviews. The key to staying sane about the impact of bad reviews is to look at the percentage they make of the total. You don't have much to worry about as long as the one and two star reviews make up one third or less of the total number of reviews. As proof, I offer the website idreambooks.com, the "Rotten Tomatoes" of the book world. They aggregate book reviews from important critics like the *New York Times* and rank best selling books according to the percentage of good reviews they got. As you explore the site, *note that the majority of best selling books have LOTS of bad reviews from important gatekeepers.*

A Bad Review Is Not An Authoritative Judgment On Your Work

The *New Yorker* magazine is arguably one of the final arbiters of literary judgment. So when its book critic James Wood trashed Donna Tartt's *The Goldfinch* as an infantile piece of drivel ("Its tone, language, and story belong in children's literature") there was room for Tartt to think, "That's it. I'm ruined as a literary author." You know, like you do when you get a bad review.

There's just one problem. For every devastating review from an authoritative arbiter of literature Tartt also received glowing ones, too. Michiko Kakutani, the chief *New York Times* book reviewer for 31 years (and a Pulitzer winner in criticism), called it "a glorious Dickensian novel, a novel that pulls together all [Tartt's] remarkable storytelling talents into a rapturous, symphonic whole. ... It's a work that shows us how many emotional octaves Ms. Tartt can now reach, how seamlessly she can combine the immediate and tactile with more wide-angled concerns."

Now, I ask you. If the *New Yorker* and the *New York Times* can't agree on the merits of the same book why on earth would you believe that any one review you get is the final judgment (positive or negative) of your book?

Remember this always: The best writers are often the ones who get the most criticism. And this: A publisher didn't choose you because you couldn't write.

Bad Reviews Can Be Good For Business

I have personally had the experience of debuting books that sold well despite initially bad reviews. How can this be? Partly, it's because *any* review is publicity. The reviewer is spreading the word about your book. Partly, it's because reviews, even if they're bad, offer "social proof" to potential buyers that somebody thought the book was worth buying. Partly, it's because sometimes the reviewer will state her dislike for something a potential buyer likes. If a shopper looks for a bleak story and the review says your dystopian fantasy sucked because it was too bleak, well, that shopper might just click on your buy button.

Sometimes poison can have medicinal value. For example, people are more likely to buy a book with bad reviews than no reviews. An Amazon book page with zero reviews gives the impression that no one wants it. A book page with a handful of bad reviews makes you ask, "Why is there such a strong reaction to this book? Maybe I should check it out."

I'm not saying bad reviews are a good thing. I'm saying they do not have nearly the power we ascribe to them.

Bad Reviews Are Often Discounted By The Public

Few people give weight to negative reviews if they are badly written, contain grammatical mistakes or fail to provide specifics.

Product reviews are everywhere, thanks to Yelp, Trip Advisor, Google Reviews, Amazon and others. Our constant exposure to them makes us better at spotting the useful from the useless. The "*I hate this book*" review, which tries to make up for its lack of specifics or coherence with CAPITAL LETTERS is simply not going to be taken seriously by most shoppers.

Bad Reviews Offer Legitimacy And Social Proof
What do you think of a book that has nothing but five-star reviews? Most of us would be suspicious. We'd think the author rallied all his friends and family to write rousing tributes. Why? Because it isn't normal for opinions to be so uniform.

Most of us *expect* to see some bad reviews. Again, check out your favorite books and see how many one-star reviews they've gotten. How can it be that David Mitchell has (as of this printing) 178 one-star reviews for *Cloud Atlas* and yet the author in our fictional example above has none? Red flag! Red flag!

In a twisted way, bad reviews give a book legitimacy because their very presence indicate that the good reviews must be genuine. Naomi Blackburn, founder of The Sisterhood of the Traveling Book, a 300+ member Goodreads group, told the Huffington Post, "Although it might sting, they [authors] want those [negative] reviews. I am leery of books that have nothing but glowing reviews."

You Aren't Writing To Make Friends
Think back to your mission, your purpose, your intention for

writing. Is it values-based like the need for self-expression? Or is it ego-based like the need to be liked, to be popular? Get on purpose with your purpose and negative reviews will stop feeling like a pterodactyl snatched you off the ground to drop you into a volcano.

Reviews Tell You More About The Reader Than About The Book.

There's no one right way to read a book. We bring our own backgrounds and experiences and opinions to what we read. Taste is notoriously subjective. As a confirmed chocolate-obsessive it boggles my mind that some people prefer vanilla over The Flavor That Gives My Life Meaning. Are the divergent opinions a statement on chocolate itself or on our taste buds?

The same could be said about book reviews. More than once I've looked at my wildly polar-hugging reviews and thought, "Did these guys read the same book? How could they come to such startlingly different conclusions?"

If you're dealing with a snide review more interested in insults than illuminations, Mary Lawrence, author of *The Alchemist's Daughter* suggests the following:

> *When you read a snarky review, replace everything that person wrote with "Look at me! I am so smart and clever unlike the idiot who wrote this book! Think less of this book and more of me!"*

Nine Healthy Ways To Dull The Pain Of Bad Reviews

When you wish upon a star you often get the pointy end in your eye. Book reviews were once the exclusive province of literary critics. Today? Everyone's a critic. As blogs, Amazon, Goodreads, NetGalley, Barnes & Noble, Apple, Google et al. take over we no longer read reviews written by editors who might offer a balanced critique of our work. Now, it's wall-to-wall snark, written by a large number of know-it-alls, wanna-be's, never-weres, trolls and haters. It is very easy for those who fail to sit in judgment of others who have not. We've gone over a lot of insights that can help you reframe a bad review, but is there any action you can take to dull the pain? Quite a few actually.

1. Dwell On Your Good Reviews

Remember what neuropsychologist Rick Hanson said: *"The brain is like Velcro for negative experiences but Teflon for positive ones."* You'd have to read a good review twice *thoroughly* for it to have the equivalent impact of *glancing* at a bad review once. So do it. Re-read your good reviews, email them to friends. Celebrate the positive the way you panic at the negative: Dwell on it, pick it apart, maximize the intensity, make it more vivid, "what-if" it ("What if this is the start of an avalanche of good reviews?!"). This is how you build a positive neural network.

2. Learn From Legitimate Critiques

Once, I angrily showed a friend a beautifully-written but highly negative critique of one of my books. My friend tried to soothe me but I wasn't having it. "I'm not hurt that he gave me a 1-star review!" I yelled. "I'm pissed off that his review is written better than my book!"

My point: A well-written critique means there's a high potential you could learn something from it for your next book. One way of determining the validity of a criticism is if it occurs frequently. For example, many reviewers said that my book *Eat It Later: Mastering Self Control & The Slimming Power Of Postponement* was, as one reviewer memorably put it, "Repetitious to the brink of making me mad." I took that to heart and cut the repetition in a later edition.

Obviously, vague, unsubstantiated claims like "this is the worst book I've ever read," aren't actionable because they don't give you enough to go on. But if the critique on your writing style, plot lines, and characterization are backed up by specific examples that resonate, then why wouldn't you take that to heart for your next book? Where else can you get that kind of honest feedback?

In his blog author Richard Levesque writes:

> *"The negative review, I've often found, is motivated by some specific thing that let the reader down…it can be helpful to try reading between the lines of those reviews, to look for the places where a book failed a reader as well as the places where a book grabbed a reader and wouldn't let go…We need to look for the reasoned, analytical, and carefully considered reviews. Those are the ones most likely to shed some real light on how a book is doing. The*

rest, treat with interest, but not as weighty deciders of one's fate."

3. Call Bullshit

Sometimes the reviewer is just plain wrong. From critiquing non-existent themes to stating factual errors, you have every right to act like a Guatemalan nanny and shake the reviewer to death. Well, in your mind, anyway. We'll talk about the wisdom of actually responding to a reviewer in a moment.

The reviewer doesn't need to state factual errors for you to raise your middle finger at him. Yes, he has the right to state an opinion of your work but you have a right to state an opinion about his review. For example, I like to sprinkle a lot of my work with entertaining stories and funny metaphors. One day I got an email from a detractor who didn't think I was funny. My response? "Screw you, clowntard. You wouldn't know funny if it bent you over and fucked you with a Coke bottle."

Okay, I didn't write that but hey, I thought it!

4. Stop Reading Them.

Author Patrick Somerville advised writers not to read any review after *New York Times* book critic Janet Maslin trashed his novel, *The Bright River*, in a mistake-riddled review. The paper actually had to print a correction to the piece. This is what Somerville wrote in salon.com:

"I've published almost two dozen books and I now read as few of my reviews as possible. Why? Because I've learned more about my work from other authors through their books, conversations, or lectures than I have from any reviewers. I don't look to reviews for education or approbation. I hope they'll help with publicity, but I've seen people get raves in the New York Times without any impact on sales. We authors shouldn't let our self-esteem be held hostage by the Janet Maslins of journalism, and we should try not to over-estimate their importance or expect them to stroke our egos."

A fair number of authors claim they don't read reviews, positive or negative. While this is certainly an option for you, I hardly think it's a viable one. It's like somebody waving a plate of homemade chocolate (CHOCOLATE!) cookies under your nose before dinner. Few could resist the temptation. Besides, how can you ignore something that seeks you out? The age of actively looking for reviews (buying a paper or magazine) has been replaced by Google Alerts that email you whenever your name or book appears on a paper, magazine or blog. Hell, I've had friends tag me on Facebook or Twitter with links to reviews.

5. Acknowledge That Your Work Is Provocative Enough To Warrant Reviews.

Never mind if they're positive or negative, the fact that you got any reviews is a sign of your relevance. I'll take trolls over silence, haters over indifference and naysayers over never-read-its any day. I'd rather know that I riled people up than to think my work was so anemic nobody could bother to buy it or write about it.

6. Get Friends To Write More Reviews

The worst part about getting a one- or two-star review on sites like Amazon or Barnes & Noble is that it sits on top of all the reviews until the next one pushes it down. I've seen this a million times, not just with my books, but the books of friends and clients. There you are with 20 great reviews but the first thing visitors to your book page see is THAT ONE AWFUL REVIEW. It's enough to make you go full-metal Nixon.

One way of dealing with it is to generate more reviews to push the bad one down and off the page. While some authors believe that getting friends and family to write reviews is unethical, I'm not one of them. It's not cheating; it's nudging.

7. Imagine Killing The Critic

Put your whodunit creativity to good use! Imagine writing a mystery/thriller in which the critic dies. The story doesn't always have to result in a pretend murder. Fictional defamation, degradation, and despoliation can be satisfying, too. No, it's not going to solve anything but neither does masturbation and look how good *that* feels.

8. Question The Agenda

Exceedingly cruel remarks—"a waste of time," or "my eight-year-old could have written a better book"—are sometimes motivated by an agenda. If it's available click the reviewer's link and read their profile. Does he favor a specific genre? Do you agree with her ratings of other books? Does she regularly review books or is this her only review? I've often felt better about a bad review when my investigations showed that the critic hated everything he ever read, including some of the classics in my genre.

9. Contact The Critic. Or Not

The conventional wisdom is that you should not ever contact a critic because you'll end up fast-tracking yourself into the Authors Behaving Badly Hall Of Fame.

First, there is a great potential to start a flame war online with a bunch of trolls who are not interested in having a respectable discussion. Second, you're liable to say something regrettable that will live online and follow you like a bird on top of a cow for the rest of your life.

I swear I didn't just call you a cow. I'm just saying that responding to reviews sounds like a lot of cud. It's like trying to advance your career by joining Scientology or getting a neck tattoo—you're going to create more problems than the problem you're trying to solve.

Yet.

There are authors who do it successfully. The hilarious writer Elle Lothlorien says she responds to each and every negative review she gets. She told *Digital Book World*, "As soon as I find out that I've gotten a bad review, I stop whatever I'm doing and run to my computer like my ass is on fire. The faster you respond, the better."

Lothlorien advises writers to stop thinking like authors and start thinking like business people. In her world, reviewers aren't readers, they're customers and urges us to apply a customer service concept universal to other industries.

Lothlorien claims that every negative review she's responded to that resulted in a dialogue (as opposed to an argument) ended up with the reviewer deleting their negative review, amending it to more favorable language or increasing their rating by at least one or two stars.

Personally, I think Lothlorien can get away with it because she's a funny, raging extrovert who could charm a banana out of a gorilla's hand. But a lot, if not most, writers are introverts. I'm not sure we're the type to do customer service very well. If you've got the personality—or the stomach—you would do well to read her advice.

You could also take Derek Murphy's advice. The founder of www.creativindie.com claims that strategic ass-kissing can help remove a bad Amazon review. He advises you to track down the reviewer's website or email and write them a short note, saying:

> *"Thanks for the review you posted for my book, I really appreciate the critical feedback because I want to become a better writer, and the thoughtful reviews like yours*

help me improve my craft and fix my writing. I'll definitely keep your thoughts in mind on future books so I don't make the same mistakes."

Murphy believes thanking people for nasty negative reviews will generally mollify them, and if you can't track them down, you should post a reply like the one above on Amazon. "It will make you look awesome even to other readers who read the nasty review and then your kind, polite response," he says.

All in all, I think it's best NOT to respond to bad reviews, unless you have the personality of a car salesman, graduated from the Ritz-Carlton School Of Customer Service or have the ability to drive a convertible through a car wash and not get wet. I am much more on AJ Truman's side. He believes that even if multiple reviewers claim you're a sexist, racist, Fill In Your Favorite-ist Here, you should not make contact:

"Being defensive about a book that's already been published doesn't work. The internet is written in ink. Those criticisms won't magically disappear because you gave a response, no matter how thoughtful. You can't change opinions. It's like thinking you can change someone's political opinion through a Facebook comment chain. What's done is done. The only thing you control is your next book."

Final Thoughts

No one wants bad reviews. They hurt. But I'm not peeing on your leg and telling you it's raining when I say they can also benefit you (in limited quantities). Negative reviews make the better reviews seem more real and they can cause controversy which can drive sales.

Let's bend toward perspective. We are writing romances, police procedurals, YA novels, historical fiction, biographies, how-to and the like. For the most part we are writing entertainment and helpful tomes. Kurt Vonnegut, recognizing that fact, once put all snarky reviewers in their place when he said, "*Any reviewer who expresses rage and loathing for a novel is preposterous. He or she is like a person who has put on full armor and attacked a hot fudge sundae.*"

Speaking of putting on full armor, many of us have to do that to keep our jealousy in check. What happens when an undeserving writer or even a deserving friend enters the white rhino'd savannah, leaving you with a bad case of poison envy?

Adjust your metal plates and codpiece because you're about to find out.

Chapter Eight

When Good Things Happen To Other Writers: Treating Poison Envy

When I first started writing one of my closest friends told me he got a six-figure book contract. I was thrilled for him, said the right words, bought him drinks, showed the right emotions. But with each smile, toast and back-slapping I died a little bit inside.

The first chance I got to be alone, I started throwing things in my apartment. It was unfair. I'd been trying for four years; he'd been trying for six months. I was totally committed to being a writer; he waffled the whole time. I took writing classes and went on writing retreats. He smoked weed and hardly touched his laptop.

As if the misery of jealousy and envy wasn't bad enough, I also had to contend with the guilt. He'd always been a good friend and here I was, not only incapable of being happy for him but berating him (in my mind and to other people). I was prick. A total prick. A jealous, envious prick.

I can't tell you how much it bothered me to play that small. I worried that not only would I lose a great friend but that I'd descend into bitterness and resentment. It took me a good while to work through the envy to get to a place where I was not only genuinely happy for him but for all friends and acquaintances who achieved more than I did. To understand how I was able to do it you first have to understand the nature of competition.

Envy As A Survival Strategy

For almost the entire history of our species we shared our resources in tribes of about 150 people or less. Did I say "share" our resources? What I really meant was compete. Your fellow tribe members were often frenemies who cooperated in some areas and competed in others. Who got more water and food when resources were scarce and had to be rationed? The strongest, the fastest, the best liked, the better hunter, the better gatherer, the one with more status. If you were going to fight somebody over food you'd better have a pretty good idea of how you'd fare in a fight, lest Hercules use your scarecrow body to light the campfire. Comparing yourself to others in the tribe, assessing yourself in relation to them helped you make decisions to stay alive.

Of course that was then and this is now. We don't compete for food or other resources for physical survival but competition is an integral part of being human even when we don't want it to be. My mom used to split the last cookie in half with the care of a diamond-cutter as my brother and I fought over who'd be "cheated." Were we "sharing" the cookie or competing for it?

Caught Between A Modern Problem & An Ancient Brain

The brain is easily highjacked by alarm and it treats social "losses" with nearly the anxiety and concern as a physical threat. My brain considered my friend's win as a two-fold danger. First, a loss of status in a tribe I called "*Writers Trying To Make It.*" I was one of its eminent leaders, as I was published in more prestigious newspapers and magazines than the other members of our group. Now, how could I lead the tribe if my friend was now the more successful one?

Second, my brain interpreted my friend's success as reducing my access to a tribe I aspired to called "*Writers Who Made It.*" That tribe accepted him and not me.

Once I understood what my brain was doing I got a much better grip on my jealousy and envy. "Ahhh," I thought. "My brain thinks I've been cast out of one tribe and blocked from joining another." I knew immediately to connect to my other tribes (friends, family, workmates) so that my brain could calm down enough for me to do some deeper work.

You Can't Choose Not To Be Envious

One of the things that really used to bother me during my bouts of envy was people telling me, "You really shouldn't feel that way," as if any of us have the power to stop thinking or feeling something at will.

Envy is an involuntary feeling. Who gets up in the morning thinking, "Today I'm going to burn with resentment and undermine my friend's success in any way I can"? Jealousy and envy are not pleasant. They are not welcome. But they're there. You can't wish it away or use will power to stop thinking about it.

In fact, trying not to be jealous is counter-productive. Thought suppression studies ("Don't think about a white bear") show the attempt to "prevent" thoughts or feelings actually generates them. Windy Dryden, Ph.D., professor of psychotherapeutic studies at Goldsmiths, University of London, confirmed that "Acknowledging envy is the first step toward taming it."

Allow The Feelings To Be There

What resists persists and what is allowed gets plowed. Envy will clop its muddy, cloven hoofs onto your living room and eat all your pretzels. Instead of denying the heifer's presence, why don't you invite it to sit for a spell? Ask yourself, "Can I allow this feeling to be here?" NO is a perfectly acceptable answer because at least it acknowledges the feeling. Still, ask yourself the same question in different ways. Like, "What would happen if I just allowed this feeling to exist for a couple of moments and nothing more?"

I'll tell you what will happen. The heifer will continue chewing on your pretzels. And while at first it's painful to have it in your living room (Gawd! The smell!) your willingness to allow it to be there will eventually be the thing that spirits it out. You see, your resistance keeps making more pretzels for the heifer to eat. The less you resist, the less pretzels you feed it and the less inclined it is to stay. ("Look, Heifer! There are yummier pretzels across the street at the home of the next writer who saw her friend get a six figure advance!")

Clomp, clomp, clomp.

Allowing your feelings to be where they are creates space. It shifts the resistance. It releases the shame. And that's when envy has a chance to move on and diffuse. You cannot let go of feelings you deny gripping.

Dig Deep To Find The Real Reason For Your Jealousy

My friend's success wasn't the cause of my envy; it was the trigger. The real source was my desperation for the success I hadn't yet experienced. Slowly, I realized envy was a way for my ego to divert attention away from everything I wanted but didn't have. Why concentrate on something that painful when I could just be mad at my friend, gossip about him in public or ridicule him in private?

Forget about trying to eliminate the feeling of envy—it's there to stay, probably for a long while. Instead, confront your shortcomings and self-doubts head on. You are not where you want to be, thought you would be or feel you should be. As long as you stare at your friend's victories you cannot address the deficits you perceive in yourself.

Honesty helped me heal from envy. Once I admitted what was really going on, I found it much easier to be around my successful friend, to hang out, to be friends and actually celebrate with him. My pain wasn't his fault. I stopped holding him responsible for it. As soon as I caught myself criticizing him in my head or to other people, I forced myself to admit that I was lashing out at my own deficiencies.

Once you own your shortcomings you may, *may* come to the

same startling conclusion I did: You are not where you want to be because you are not who you need to become.

How To Use Envy As A Change Agent

Psychologists divide envy into two major categories: Malignant and benign. Malignant envy makes you wish failure on others and get pleasure in their suffering. Benign envy simply makes you want to replicate the success you're witnessing without causing harm to the successful.

Malignant envy makes you think, "*Your book is on the best seller list and mine is digging tunnels? Die, BITCH, DIE!*" Benign envy makes you think, "*If SHE can do it so can I!*" In this way, envy can be a positive, motivating force.

Social comparison has the power to drive us or divide us. The difference between experiencing benign and malignant envy seems to be whom we're comparing ourselves to. If we compare ourselves to somebody we can identify with (same social status, same intelligence level) who worked hard, and took a path that seems doable to us, envy tends to be benign with a high likelihood of being a positive motivating force. It can make us believe in ourselves more and help us work harder at success.

For example, envy might result in a positive change in your own behavior if a writer you admire gained white rhino success as a consequence of skipping late night parties so she could get up at 5:00 am to write her novel. Her example might prompt you to stop being a lazy cat in a dog-eat-dog world.

Tame The Envy By Comparing Yourself To The Appropriate Writers

We can't help but compare. We're comparing machines. Go to the gym and you'll compare your body to other people. Go to work and you'll compare the size of your office. We can't not compare, so why not do it with the two types of writers that can do you some good:

1. Somebody With Similar Or Slightly Better Writing Skills. If you make an upward comparison to a literary great rather than someone with a similar skill set you'll be discouraged beyond reckoning ("I'll never write that well so why even try?"). If I wrote subversive narrative, for example, Chuck Palhaniuk might be an appropriate literary hero but a completely inappropriate object of envy.

2. The Person Staring Back At You In The Mirror Studies show that one of the best ways to harness the power of comparison is to do a side-by-side analysis of your own career. It's true that you don't have the success that you *want*, but it's probably true that you're way ahead of where you were a year, or two or five ago. One author I know despaired over the fact that her latest book didn't get a starred review. I reminded her that a few years ago she was thrilled that Publishers Weekly reviewed her book at all. "I know," she said. "But I'm looking for progress." I replied, "Progress is going from not getting *any* book reviewed by Publishers Weekly to getting *all* of them reviewed." She just sort of just blinked at me as she absorbed the reframe. It's important to acknowledge how far you've come, even if you haven't yet arrived.

It's perfectly normal to compare yourself against others by looking through the windshield to see who's ahead and the side-view mirrors to see who's around. But it's just as helpful to look in the rear-view mirror to see how far you've come.

Discover The Problems Of People You're Jealous Of

Who do you want to destroy with your patented Death Glare? Before you activate the laser beam, find out what they've had to deal with in their lives. You might be surprised by their problems and weaknesses. Perhaps they grew up poor, were physically or sexually abused, or struggled with dyslexia or stuttered throughout their childhood.

For instance, the writer friend I was so jealous of. I found out by accident that his father committed suicide when he was a teen. Worse, his father had called him right before he killed himself, so my friend has carried the burden of guilt ever since. Envy tends to blur your vision of the successful. You end up thinking they're successful at everything or that their life is easy. I'm not saying pity is the answer to envy. Just that it's much easier to rejoice in somebody else's victories when you see their full humanity, not just their super-hero author status.

Learn From The People You're Jealous Of

Being jealous should make you pay attention, listen carefully, watch observantly, and take notes. If you envy somebody's thrilling writing style, buy their books and dissect their sentences as if they were frog parts in Biology 101. If you're jealous of their confidence and charm in writing groups or networking situations, then study them at a cocktail party. If you envy the creativity of their ideas, ask them about their process. The best people to learn from are the people you're jealous of.

Get Clear On Your Purpose

One of the best ways to short-circuit the green-eyed monster is to reconnect to your purpose. Why are you writing? Is it for the advance? The prestige? The parties? Seeing your name on bestseller lists? These are all nice and who wouldn't want them but are they at the core of what you want or at the margins? Don't re-double your efforts after losing sight of the objective.

Most writers have a voice longing to be heard. Most writers want to add value to other people's lives. They want to make people laugh, think, commiserate, and love. What does this have to do with starred reviews from Publishers Weekly, six-figure advances or making the best seller lists? Those are great add-ons to the car but are they the engine that drives it? Get clear on your purpose and the motor-mouthed green-eyed monster will be at a loss for words.

Cultivate Generosity

One way to stop being small is to play big. I used to be a contributing writer to salon.com when it was the Internet's Big Deal. The editor asked me to write on a topic I wasn't particularly interested in nor suited for. I told her I didn't think I was right for the piece but knew someone who was. So, what did I do? I recommended the writer friend I was so jealous of!

This was before anyone knew my friend got a big advance so I basically introduced him to a national audience. He was genuinely excited and authentically grateful, which helped me get in touch with why I liked my friend to begin. Later, when he got more famous he got me in as a regular commentator on NPR's All Things Considered. My generosity led to his kindness which tempered my envy. It proved the Chinese proverb that "A bit of fragrance always clings to the hand that gives you roses."

You can't always make a kind gesture like that to somebody who's more successful than you are but you can do it for others. My motto, born out of seeing the destructive power of jealousy and the cleansing effects of generosity, is simple: Help Another Writer.

Avoid People Who Enable Or Encourage Your Jealousy

It's important to avoid writers who habitually value the wrong things. If you spend all your time with authors who cackle about who's zooming who, you're going to constantly evaluate yourself in the wrong way. If you spend all your time with writers who talk about their advances, their Amazon ranking and their royalties you are going to fall into the inevitable trap of comparing your status to theirs. Change the subject or remove yourself from the conversation (or the relationship). Instead, hang out with writers who talk about writing and the things that drive your purpose.

The Power And Folly Of Social Comparisons

Bertrand Russell once said, "*If you desire glory, you may envy Napoleon, but Napoleon envied Caesar, Caesar envied Alexander, and Alexander, I daresay, envied Hercules, who never existed.*" Russell's point: Everybody gets jealous but if you don't rein it in you'll end up envious of fictional characters.

Whether it's Napoleon envying Caesar or a pokey writer like me envying a white rhino like my friend, it's normal to make interpersonal comparisons to evaluate ourselves, enhance our self esteem and improve our status. Positive, too, in some ways. Nothing will motivate you to run faster than somebody who zips by you. Or jump further than somebody who flings past you. How can you tell if your book is doing well unless you look at other books like it on Amazon's ranking?

The problem with social comparisons is that they often end up making you feel inadequate. Our goal as writers is to stay on the positive side of the envy spectrum, to make it work for us instead of against us. And if we can't, then we need to root out the real causes of our envy.

I had a choice with my writer friend who found white rhino success. He got something I wanted and didn't have. Would I become resentful and lose a friendship or make peace with the way things are?

I chose peace and worked my way toward it by facing my own sense of inadequacy. That doesn't mean I stopped feeling envious instantly; I still desperately wanted to have what my friend had.

But separating the source of my envy from the friend who triggered it made it possible for me to practice what Buddhists call "Mudita"—finding vicarious joy in the good fortune of others.

Being able to manage envy is a crucial part of constructing a bulletproof consciousness. Now that we've begun to silence the voice of the green-eyed monster there's another voice we have to address and it's the one in your head.

What are we going to do about your inner critic?

Chapter Nine

Managing The Biggest Critic Of All: YOU

The obstacles before us pale in comparison to the obstacles within us. In past chapters we've seen how a bulletproof consciousness can turn poison into medicine but here our powers will be tested for there is no more potent poison than the one coursing between our ears.

One of the confounding things about dealing with your inner critic is that it simultaneously lifts and undermines you. Your inner critic is the CEO of Quality Control. It senses when you've written garbage. It knows when you've cut corners. By holding you to a higher standard it maximizes your chances of success while protecting you from public shame and humiliation.

The problem is that our inner critic often does it with all the warmth of a serial killer. We *need* our inner critic. What we don't need is for it to be so hateful.

And bi-polar. The inner critic is both a knight in shining armor that rescues us from mediocrity and a vampire that sucks on its own neck. And sometimes, just to fuck with us, the vampire dresses up in the knight's armor, galloping in to save the day but spilling our blood in the process.

The bulletproof consciousness knows that its inner critic has a split personality and that the knight (which treats us kindly) must be fed and the vampire (which hates us) starved. We can start by understanding that psychologists see self-criticism as a "safety behavior," a badly formulated attempt to protect ourselves from painful situations, memories and emotions. All that self-monitoring, self-blaming and self-criticism you're doing is actually serving an important function: Keeping you safe from physical or emotional harm.

Wait, how does being mean to yourself keep you safe? Well, let's say an agent turns you down because he asked for a one-page synopsis and you sent him the whole manuscript. In order to make sure you never do something like that again, you might berate yourself into behaving better ("I'm such an idiot! Can't I listen?!"). Browbeating, as many browbeaters can attest, is actually an effective way to prevent yourself from making errors.

It's also a highly effective way to destroy your self-esteem.

Self-persecution can also serve as a punishment to deter you from repeating mistakes. Let's say you ate a big piece of chocolate cake (CHOCOLATE!). You call yourself a fat pig and sentence yourself to three hours at the gym. That'll teach you to say NO next time! As many of us who've done this can attest, flogging yourself works in the short term but it also leaves emotional scars resistant to healing.

Think of your self-criticism as a means to an end. A perverse, but effective way to achieve your goal. Want to wake up earlier to work on your novel? Call yourself lazy and threaten to cancel your vacation unless you do it three times this week.

Want to get a bigger advance? Call yourself a pussy for not asking more the last time and insult yourself into being more demanding.

Want your editor to like your next manuscript? Tell yourself you're a lousy writer and if you don't burn the midnight oil your editor is going to unmask you for the impostor you really are. That'll get you to work harder. All this brings up a great question: Why do we believe we can only be motivated by hateful self-talk?

Psychologists who study self-criticism say it's because we're driven by fear. Their research led to an unmistakable conclusion: We take on high levels of self-cruelty because we think it's the best way of winning and protecting ourselves from loss. Psychologists use a questionnaire to understand why we talk to ourselves the way we do and they've split their patients' answers into four major categories:

1. Preventing Shame & Humiliation

- "To prevent future embarrassments."
- "To remind me of my past failures."
- "To keep me from making minor mistakes."

2. Achievement

- "To make sure I keep up my standards."
- "To make me concentrate."
- "To remind me of my responsibilities."

- "To show I care about my mistakes."

3. Self-Regulation

- "To keep myself in check."
- "To stop me being angry with others."
- "To stop me being lazy."
- "To gain reassurance from others."
- "To stop me becoming arrogant."
- "To stop myself being happy."

4. Punishment

- "Because, if I punish myself I feel better."
- "To harm part of myself."
- "To take revenge on part of myself."
- "To punish myself for my mistakes."
- "To cope with feelings of disgust with myself."
- "To destroy a part of me."
- "To get at the things I hate in myself."

As you can see, we use the bad (loathsome self-talk) to achieve the good (high performance and self-protection). Self-criticism provides safety, self-regulation and motivation. It keeps us alert to errors, and protects us from criticism, rejection, shame and humiliation. This is a good thing. But you can do a good thing in a bad way. In order to change we must ask ourselves a few questions:

- Is self-persecution the only path to self-protection?
- Is self-flagellation the only way to overcome laziness?
- Are insults the only path to motivation?
- What is the point of protecting yourself from humiliation if it ends up leaving you in a puddle of self-hate?

It's possible to achieve the noble goals of self-criticism—achievement, self-protection, better work—without using its means, but it requires us to use a different type of motivation.

Shifting Your Focus From Fear Of Loss To Anticipation Of Gain

Fear of loss drives the inner critic into the arms of cruelty. Expectation of gain drives us into the bosom of kindness. Fear of loss uses insulting, coercive tactics. Expectation of gain uses uplifting, inviting methods. Both accomplish the same goals but leave you in radically different states. One leaves you cowed and demoralized; the other hopeful and energized. If you want to stop hateful self-talk you first have to recognize that you're operating out of fear, not hope.

In fact, most of us operate out of fear because the brain is wired for negativity. As explained before, the brain is far more sensitized to sticks than to carrots. In fact, it is so attuned to fear and loss that it often overcomes reason and logic.

Dr. Daniel Kahneman, a professor at Princeton, was awarded the Nobel Prize in economics (quite a feat since he is a psychologist!). Through his work in "loss aversion" he showed an asymmetry between gains and losses that causes a psychological myopia in people's behavior. The central notion in "loss aversion" is this: Losing something is more painful than getting something is pleasurable. We may like to win but we *hate* to lose.

Kahneman's studies show that we typically fear loss twice as much as we relish success. As he told the *New York Times*: "In my classes I say, 'I'm going to toss a coin, and if it's tails, you lose $10. How much would you have to gain on winning in order for this gamble to be acceptable to you?'"

Students typically want more than $20 before the bet becomes acceptable to them. Kahneman, along with most economists, believes this is ridiculous. Losing $10 shouldn't be any more painful than gaining $10 is pleasurable. But it is. People, and by people I mean you and me, are highly loss averse.

How Loss Aversion Applies To Writers

Kahneman's model explains why established writers—midlisters and bestsellers—actually experience more pain when they get rejected than newbies trying to break in. According to his theory, the misery of getting kicked out of the writing tribe is twice as painful as the pleasure of getting in. Loss aversion also convinced us writers that the inner critic's voice must be vicious if it is to be effective.

How To Change Our Inner Critic's Voice Without Sacrificing Performance

Fear distorts our ability to make good decisions. It made you decide that cruelty is a great way of avoiding loss. But once you realize that you're operating out of a fear of failure rather than a will to win you can start making better decisions. Like changing the tone of your inner critic so it lifts rather than demeans. Here's how:

1. Stop Beating Yourself Up For Beating Yourself Up

Don't criticize yourself for being self-critical. First of all, you're not "doing it;" it's doing you. You're wired for loss aversion. You don't consciously wake up every morning and say, "Today, I'm going to torture myself with insults to avoid the loss I'm fearing."

2. Don't Refute The Subject Of Your Self Criticism With Evidence

Don't try to talk yourself out of something that may be true. Are you bullying yourself because it helps stop you from being lazy? Then don't deny your laziness. We're not trying to change what you're being critical about, just the way you frame the criticism. The challenge isn't to make the case for or against your laziness; the challenge is in seeing if there's a warmer, more caring and compassionate way to overcome it.

3. Address The Underlying Fears

Your subconscious will be very reluctant to give up self-criticism if you don't work on the fear that's driving it. When you toil in a rejection-prone world like publishing, self-criticism can motivate you to work hard, keep your negative emotions in check and earn a place in the industry. If you gave up self-criticism you might not work so hard, not spot your mistakes and thus never find a place where people love or value you. It's the fear of rejection that's driving the self-criticism. Learning to recognize your self-persecution as fear-based and being compassionate about that fear will gradually reduce the hostility of your self-attacks.

4. Face Your Fears With Compassion

The word compassion literally means to "suffer with." So the first step toward self-compassion is to *notice* that you're suffering. You're actually suffering in two ways— by experiencing the fears and anxieties that are driving the self-criticism and then the savagery of the self-criticism itself.

Kristin Neff, a pioneer in the field of self-compassion research conducts an interesting experiment during her seminars. She has people pair up and sit across from each other. Imagine you're one of them. Your partner is asked to close her eyes while you are asked to sit and look at her through a loving-kindness meditation. You inevitably feel warmth and compassion toward her.

Then it's your turn to close your eyes. You feel her eyes on you. You get uncomfortable. You hear a voice saying, "I don't deserve compassion. I yell at the kids. I didn't stand up to my editor. I... Fill In The Blank."

After the exercise Neff asks the crowd how many found it easier to generate compassion for a complete stranger than for themselves. Almost everybody's hands go up. Neff believes there are a couple of reasons we do this:

We Equate Self-Compassion With Self-Indulgence
We conflate being nice with being lenient. We think we're getting away with something but are we? Self-compassion is about your health and well-being. Self-indulgence is simply about gratification of one's appetites despite the consequences.

We Will Fail Unless We Criticize Ourselves
This gets at the heart of self-criticism—that without out it we won't be able to motivate ourselves. Is that true? We know it isn't true for other people so why is it true for us? You wouldn't hand a whip to a child and say, "Here, motivate yourself with a few lashes!" The motivational power of compassionate self-talk is based on the anticipation of gain not the fear of loss. Yes, you can motivate yourself with fear (and you have), but you can also succeed without it. Flip the frame and ask yourself: "Do I need to be mean to myself in order to get what I want?" If the answer is yes then ask yourself another question: "Am I *willing* to get what I want without attacking myself?"

It's Selfish Or Weak To Be Compassionate To Yourself
Our thought process goes something like this: "Why am I thinking about myself when I could be thinking of and helping others? I'm a selfish prick! And why am I being such a sissy about a few tough moments, anyway?" This line of thinking is easily debunked by,

of all things, the airline industry. What's the first thing they tell you to do during an in-flight emergency? THINK OF YOURSELF FIRST. You are to put the oxygen mask on yourself before you put one on your child. Not out of selfishness but out of service. Without putting it on yourself first you might black out before you get it on your child! That's not selfish; that's about making yourself strong to strengthen other people.

5. Develop Compassion For Yourself

It's one thing to know you need to practice self-compassion, it's another to know how to do it. Use this guide:

Close your eyes and think about the last time your inner voice was cruel.

For example, you might have said this to yourself the last time you worked on a manuscript: "I'm as creative as a bowl of waxed apples. The characters in my story are one dimensional. I don't care if I have to bleed it out of myself I'm not moving my fat ass off this chair until I develop richer portraits."

Ask yourself, "What was I trying to accomplish?"

Remember, your self-criticism is a means to an end. It's always seeking to activate something good or prevent something bad (see the above list if you're stumped).

Example: "I want to improve the quality of my work."

Ask yourself, "What am I afraid will happen if I don't accomplish my goal?"
Example: "My editor will reject my manuscript."

Ask yourself, "What consequences will I suffer if I fail?"
Example: "I will lose out on an advance I was planning to pay bills with. I will lose my status as a successful author, I will lose respect from my peers. I will be publicly humiliated."

Acknowledge the reality.
Say to yourself: "These are the real reasons I'm so hard on myself—because I don't want any of these things to happen to me."

Place both hands over your heart. Notice your fears. Be with them.
Don't try to get rid of them. Suffering is pain. Extraordinary suffering is pain + resistance.

Visualize an amber, golden light surrounding your fear.
Picture the light bathing your fears with kindness and compassion. It is a visual hug to let your fears know you see them, feel them and are listening to them without judgment. It is not compassion's job to get rid of the fear. Its job is to sit with the suffering and offer it a shoulder to lean on. It is to respect the fear and offer it the solace of understanding. Sit with whatever emotions stir in you until you've come to a natural resting space.

This is an especially important point so let me repeat: Trying to make pain go away with self-compassion is just another way of repressing it. Compassion is not a solution for your problems any more than it is when you extend it to a friend. For example, being compassionate to a fellow writer whose publishing contract didn't get renewed will make them feel better but it will not get them another publishing contract. Compassion is about creating a safe space for emotions to be expressed and processed without judgment. This reduces suffering, which then leaves you or your friend stronger to face what awaits.

6. Toggle Between Fear Of Failure And Pleasure Of Winning

Now that you've faced your fear and soothed it with compassion I want you to pick up a coin and look at it. Pretend "tails" is the fear of loss and "heads" is the pleasure of gain.

Now take the coin and place it on a table heads up, symbolizing your conscious choice to operate out of a will to win rather than a fear of loss. Pick it up again and look at the tails side. Notice the contours of the fear. Flip it again and notice the texture of the pleasure. Toggle between the two so that you can see that both elements make up the coin.

Now, think of something you're struggling with. For example, getting up early to finish your manuscript.

As you think about your inability or unwillingness to wake up early, place the coin on the table with "tails" up, signifying that you're operating out of loss aversion. How does your inner critic language the problem? It might be: "*If I don't wake up early and finish my manuscript I won't get the second half of my advance, which means I can't afford to go on vacation so I better get off my fat lazy ass and set the alarm.*"

Now, flip the coin on the table so that it's "heads up" signifying that you're operating out of the pleasure of gaining. How does your inner critic language the problem? It might be: "*If I wake up early and finish my manuscript I'll get the second half of my advance which means I'll soon be sipping margaritas by the beach. I better set the alarm if I want to get my drunk on!*"

You're at choice. Do you want to motivate yourself out of loss or gain?

7. Consciously Choose Desire Over Your Subconscious Pull Toward Aversion

Pull out a coin. I have one on my desk and I take it out whenever my inner critic bares its fangs. I place the coin tails up signifying my current feelings—that I'm operating out of loss aversion. I then acknowledge the fears driving my feelings (instead of resisting them or trying to make them go away) and generate compassion for myself. When my fears recede to a manageable level I flip the coin so that it's "heads up," symbolizing my desire to be motivated by the anticipation of gain rather than the fear of loss.

I then concentrate on what I can attain instead of what I can lose and say some form of this: "I respect my fear but I choose to operate out of my will to win." And then I reframe whatever fear-based insult I assaulted myself with more empowering self-talk.

Making Your Inner Critic Work For You Not Against You

The bulletproof consciousness knows the goal isn't to gag the inner critic but to improve its ability to empower us. The next time you beat yourself up (and there's always a next time) think back to this exercise, to the acknowledgement of your fears, your ability to offer self-compassion, to your brain's natural default to loss aversion and then to the fact that there is a different way to motivate yourself.

You may be wired to fear loss but you're meant to win big.

Chapter Ten

The Folly Of Trying To Learn From Your Failures

What could be wrong with trying to make sense of your failures and rejections? If you know why something happened or didn't happen you can build strategies around it to either repeat the success or avoid the failure. Cognitive psychologists and communication theorists call it "Sense making," and they see it as an integral part of learning. But as you'll soon see, it does not apply to writers.

Sense making is valuable in large organizations where ideas and data are enthusiastically shared with others in an effort solve problems, disseminate information, build consensus and chart a way forward. But we writers don't get empirical data from publishers or work in a sharing culture with forthcoming people. Sense making offers relief to *organizations* but rarely to individuals. So, yes, Simon & Schuster gets a lot out of sense making from their failures but *you and I* won't. Indeed, studies of individual (as opposed to organizational) sense making shows it isn't just fruitless but harmful because it creates so much anxiety and frustration.

Let's say you're a fairly accomplished author with several books under her belt. But your last couple of books didn't do so well, and you editor seems a bit soured by that. She rejects your new manuscript with a mystifying opacity. Should you go on a sense making mission? Certainly, you should try to get more details out of her but in the end it won't help much. Here's why: All you'll get out of it is her opinion, which may or may not be correct.

Publishing isn't an industry like engineering where hard truths eat soft opinions without so much as a resulting burp. If your new air conditioner design gets rejected because you broke the laws of ventilation that's fixable. But in writing? Please. There are no truths, only opinions. Informed opinions to be sure, but opinions nonetheless. For example, this is what Stephen King found out when he tried to make sense of early rejection letters for *Carrie*: Some editors thought it wasn't scary enough!

This is one of the problems of sense making in publishing—finding out why you failed carries the potential of harming you. Imagine if Stephen King had "learned from his failure" and changed one of the scariest books of all time!

Again, it is relatively easy to learn from your mistakes if you're in the hard sciences. Like gravity, if something works it works all the time. If something doesn't work it will always not work. If you mix blue with yellow it will always produce green. *Always.*

This is not true in publishing. There are no laws, only shape-shifting suggestions and unpredictable results. In publishing, if I mix blue and yellow I might get green but you might get pink and another author might get purple.

If you and I have strikingly similar books and take the identical approach to marketing, publicity and advertising we will get strikingly different results. This is why it's useless to ask a success-ful author why they're successful. They might attribute their success to their agent. So you get the same agent and nothing happens. They might attribute success to their blog. So you start a blog and nothing happens. They might attribute success to a particular writing process. You adopt that process and nothing happens. The successful author mixed blue with yellow to get green. You mixed the exact same colors and got white.

And that, in a nutshell is why it's so hard to learn from your fail-ures as a writer—because there are no hard "laws" in publishing to measure them against. A mistake for you might be the solution for another author. A solution for another author might be a mistake for you. The same "mistake" you make on one book could be the breakthrough for your next.

Because much of the reasons for our failures are unknowable, the search for the truth, the desire to learn from our mistakes, isn't just an exercise in futility; it's a recipe for emotional chaos. Indeed, studies show that people who seek a reason for their loss are no happier than the people who didn't seek an answer at all. Think about that for a minute. Science says you will be happier if you don't try to make sense of a failure. Why? Researchers believe that sense making, in the absence of facts, creates more oppor-tunities for agitation, anxiety, rumination, circular thinking and obsessive behavior. And in publishing there are few facts. There are no conclusions to be had, only conjectures to be mulled.

Making Sense Out Of Crappy But Successful Writers.

Publishing is one of the few industries that regularly elevates the minimally talented to the top of their professions. Surgeons unfamiliar with sutures don't win Surgeon Of The Year. CFO's don't get promoted for being able to add two plus two. Physicists don't advance by writing books like *Subtraction: Addition's Tricky Friend.*

But that's not true in publishing. Cruise through some of Amazon's best seller lists and prepare for your inner Ann Coulter to come out. How could so much drivel sell so well? You will shoulder-roll past your belief in fairness at 700 MPH.

This is crazy-making, writer style. I for one have no problem seeing a well-written book succeed but I turn rabid when I see crappy books take up oxygen at the upper stratosphere of the bestseller lists. It drives me up the wall but trying to make sense of it just puts me deeper into the wall. Why? Because there are no real answers; only guesses that lead to suppositions. In almost every other area of my life, there is a huge benefit to "making sense" out of things I don't understand. If I can't float on the lake I ask people who can and what they tell me helps me float. If I ask a shitty writer how they shot to the top of the charts it helps me do nothing except rage at God.

Trying to make sense of your misfortune or an unworthy competitor's fortune is a proven way of distressing yourself. You might as well spray Calm-Be-Gone all over your body. Yes, it's always useful to find out what you could have done better so that you can adapt for your next effort, but good luck trying to get *accurate* or actionable information.

To be fair, *sometimes* you really can get a slice of useful information. If enough editors deem your manuscript "confusing" then you might, MIGHT want to change it. But I remind you that many editors thought James Joyce and J.R.R. Tolkien were confusing, too.

Learning From Mistakes vs. Learning To Go Forward

Always talk to trusted people with experience—your agent, your editor, your writing friends (especially your *successful* writing friends). Don't dwell on the WHY or WHY NOT of a misfortune, ask them the HOW and WHAT of moving forward. Read books, articles and blogs. Pay attention to book marketing experts, go to seminars and writing retreats. Don't try to make sense out of a senseless industry. You'll just tie yourself into a pretzel.

So You Can't Learn Anything From Your Failures?

Under certain conditions, it is possible for writers to learn from their failures. Certainly, it's easy to learn from procedural mistakes. You got rejected because the agent asked for a short synopsis and you sent the whole manuscript. Lesson learned: Follow directions.

You hated the cover your publisher came up with but didn't voice your opinion because you didn't want to rock the boat. The hideous beast comes out and sales hit the floor. Lesson learned: Speak up.

You're a self-pubbed author and you didn't analyze the best dimensions for your POD book. It comes out and the size is dorky for the genre. Lesson learned: Never rush an important decision.

But those are more like "life lessons" that anybody in any industry can glean from their failures. So, yes, you can learn from your failures *as long as there are factual reasons behind them.*

Learn It Later

Engineer and writer Ben Mordecai believes there's little to learn from failure—at least in the short term. There's much to recommend in his advice to let time and self-reflection reveal bigger truths:

> *You can learn something... later. A lot of [learning-from-failure clichés] emphasize all the ways you can fail again and learn something again and that's a great concept, but the reality is that the lessons you learn from failure aren't for you to learn immediately. If your decisions, habits, and mindsets are what caused the failure, what makes you think that you're going to be properly able to change your thinking and take home a lesson just because you failed? A better idea is to take a few pictures that day and write down a few thoughts. You're going to stew over this for a little while, but as time goes on, you are going to realize what really happened, and you're going to get that lesson that all the TED talks have promised you.*

Don't Learn From Your Failures. Exploit Them.

Like many who've succeeded in publishing, I didn't learn from my mistakes; I capitalized on them. Over time I learned to see failure as a *barrier necessary for success.* We know from the Nio Statues that only the strong survive the journey but how do you *get* strong? By being tested, not feted. By pitting yourself against something stronger than you are. Barriers you can't surmount. Obstacles you can't get past.

For example, barbells and weights are barriers you must overcome to build muscle. You must lift the barrier off you to gain muscle. Therefore, the *barrier is necessary for your success.* Alex Lickerman, MD, in his awesome book, *The Undefeated Mind: On The Science of Constructing An Indestructible Self,* puts it this way:

> *Action almost always elicits resistance from our surroundings because people, places, and things are saturated with inertia and reflexively resist change. The wise, however, know not only to anticipate such obstacles, but also to welcome them, recognizing barriers not only as inevitable but also as precursors to success.*

By way of example, Lickerman notes a huge problem engineers faced when they first designed planes. Speed is necessary to get lift-off but the more speed the plane picks up the more wind resistance it encounters. Engineers didn't 'learn' anything from the wind. They exploited it. They shaped the wings to take advantage of the resistance and voila! Up, up and away!

The barrier was necessary for success.

That is how you learn from failure in publishing—by exploiting it. By using the barriers to make you strong or by using them to catapult you into success. What's an example? Self-publishing. Sensations like Barry Eisler and J.A Konrath "shaped their wings" over publishing's resistance and flew to new heights.

What's another example? Every writer who used their anger at the industry's unfairness to push themselves toward success.

Another example? Writers who succeeded in one genre after failing in another.

Another example? Writers who discovered they were better screenwriters than novelists as a result of all the barriers they encountered.

Another example? Mediocre writers who became great writers precisely because so many publishers rejected them. They used their failures as prompts to improve their craft.

Using Failure As A Path To Success

You want to get to the top of a mountain. There's no map but the locals say it only takes an hour. Sixty minutes later you're nowhere near the top. Have you failed?

Yes.

How will trying to learn from failure help you? If you backtrack you'd just be guessing at where you went wrong. Why not use failure to chart a new course?

Failure brought you to a view of the top you didn't have before.

Is that a goat trail leading up the mountain? That could well be your path up, but you wouldn't have seen it without first making mistakes.

Instead of berating yourself for your lack of direction, your failure to read a compass, or ruminate about how you always do that or how this always happens to you, *look up*. There might be a route that wasn't apparent before.

There are three things I want to emphasize here. First, the path to victory can't be planned, it can only be discovered. Second, failure is the fastest way to discovery. Third, take the bad things you discover and instead of "learning from your mistakes," create value out of them. Exploit them. Failures let you see the road to success from a different vantage point than you started with. If you look hard enough, you might just see a path to the top.

Chapter Eleven

At It For Years With Little To Show For It? Dealing With Chronic Frustration

Success has eluded you after years of trying. You work hard, produce good work and zip, zilch, nada. Well maybe not nada but you're nowhere near where you thought you would or should be. Years of frustration and disappointment have dug tunnels in your fortitude, leaving quarries in your outlook.

Maybe you're a newbie who can't break in after a year of trying. Or a midlister who's career stalled after years of accomplishments. Or a best seller who can't replicate the success of earlier books and fears a long slide toward irrelevance. You struggle against cynicism and despair. You dismiss new ideas ("I already tried that!"), people who try to help ("I already tried that!"), and new directions ("I already tried that!").

You're caught in a vicious circle of frustration, resentment, and despair. This goes beyond dealing with any individual rejection; it's now a state of mind that you're dealing with, a narrative that says you could star in The Biggest Loser, Author Edition.

How do you get out of this vicious circle? First, by reminding yourself that publishing is unlike any other industry. There is no justice. There is no peace. There is no fairness. As Elizabeth Gilbert writes in *Big Magic*:

"The Patron goddess of creative success can sometimes seem like a rich, capricious old lady who lives in a giant mansion on a distant hill and who makes really weird decisions about who gets her fortune. She sometimes rewards charlatans and ignores the gifted. She cuts people out of her will who loyally served her for their entire lives, and then gives a Mercedes to that cute boy who cut her lawn once. She changes her mind about things. We try to divine her motives, but they remain occult. She is never obliged to explain herself to us."

Indeed. Without acknowledging the nature of success in publishing (it is exceedingly mysterious and unfair) you are destined to drown in a vat of cynicism and despair.

Once you fully absorb the concept that publishing decisions are allegorically made by that wealthy, batty lady well on her way to Alzheimer's, the knife edge of frustration gets dulled just enough to give you some wiggle room to entertain some other ideas.

Like your purpose.

Let's revisit our conversation about why you write. Is it to make a lot of money? To get great reviews? To be loved by strangers? To see your name up in lights? Yes, who wouldn't want these things but I didn't ask what you wanted; I asked about something much bigger.

What Is Your Purpose?

I'm going to go out on a limb and say that while you *want* the money, the fame, and the respect, those are merely the condiments that make your purpose taste better. If those things were your purpose then you wouldn't care how or what you did to achieve them. You can achieve fame and fortune as an orange-haired real estate developer or as a car parts manufacturer.

But you didn't choose other fields; you chose writing. And there are reasons for that. For most writers, it's to express their thoughts, communicate their feelings and release their imaginations. It's to voice their passions, to provide value for other people, to *decant their souls*, to gift humanity with the flowers of possibility.

We writers share the same purpose that drives all creative people: An innate, compulsive, irresistible, urgent need TO CREATE.

Have you failed on that score?

No. You've succeeded, and in many cases brilliantly. *Even if your manuscripts never got published.* Every unpublished manuscript is a purpose realized—a manifestation of the divine, urgent need TO CREATE.

It doesn't matter if your manuscript was published or whether it was and it succeeded or failed. Wasn't it fun? Challenging? Didn't it peak your curiosity? Demand discipline? Encourage your creativity? Give voice to your innermost thoughts and feelings? Didn't it make your imagination soar? Didn't you get a thrill out of creating something from nothing?

Then you've succeeded at your purpose.

Elizabeth Gilbert has something important to say in this matter. She turns the cliché question of "what would you do if you knew you couldn't fail" into a much more profound inquiry: What do you feel strongly enough about doing that you would do it even if you were *guaranteed to fail?*

She uses this question to drive a point about purpose. When you live out of your purpose outcome doesn't matter. "Failure" and "success" become irrelevant. You cannot measure the act of creating, of being creative, of having created with outcomes like money or fame.

Stand On Your Purpose & Frustration Will Take A Seat

This is how you deal with the chronic frustration of not "succeeding" in publishing—you remind yourself why you're doing what you're doing. And if you doubt your purpose you clarify it by asking yourself these questions:

"Am I willing to stop creating because I'm not getting the response I want?"

"If I could get money and prestige in another industry would I stop writing?"

"If I got offered money to stop writing would I take it?"

If you wavered on these questions you might consider pulling the plug on your PC, at least for a while, until a stronger intent wells up. But most of us would answer these questions with a "HELL NO."

When you live out of your purpose frustration won't leave the room but it will take a seat. Our aim isn't to make normal human emotions like frustration go away; it's to manage them and reduce the intensity so they don't cloud our purpose.

You were put on this earth to create. The outcome cannot matter.

Chapter Twelve

Radical Gratitude
A Counter-Intuitive Approach
To Building Resiliency

Gratitude, the art of appreciating what you have rather than lamenting what you don't, is an important part of the bulletproof consciousness. When it works it's an empowering way to take your mind off rejection.

When it works.

Personally, I have a big problem with gratitude and it's probably the same one you've got: It feels great for about a minute and then you're right back where you started. Gratitude is easy to practice when things are going well; almost impossible when they're not. In fact, when things are not going well, it's as useless as a bottle of booze at a Mormon wedding.

I've always felt like I had my nose pressed against the window, witnessing all the shiny, happy Oprah-infused people practicing gratitude every day, wondering why it seemed to work for everyone but me. Then I discovered a lot of fellow noses pressed against that window. And some of those noses belonged to academic researchers wondering why so many studies fail to show positive effects to practicing gratitude.

You read that right. Many studies on gratitude show it is ineffective in lifting mood. In a study looking at "gratitude tests" published in the *Journal Of Personality & Social Psychology* researchers concluded that the scientific evidence for the gratitude hypothesis is mixed and inconsistent. "The mixed bag of results," the paper said, "Suggests that the effects of thinking about positive life events are not well understood."

Given that the research is inconclusive, is there a place for gratitude in the bulletproof consciousness? Yes, if we practice it in a radically different way than we're used to. First, let's understand why…

The Way You Practice Gratitude Doesn't Work Very Well.

Researchers believe there may be a couple of rational explanations for the mixed results in their studies. The first is a psychological phenomenon called habituation, which basically desensitizes you to an event, relationship, a product or anything that you're in constant contact with. For example, it's easy to be grateful for your new iPhone—until it becomes such an intrinsic part of your daily life that you hardly notice it. At that point we start focusing on other things—things we DON'T have. The same is true for people, jobs, experiences and events. We start pining for what we don't have because we've habituated to what we do.

The standard way to practice gratitude is to think about the *presence* of positive events or people. Having an awesome spouse, or kid, watching your team win the Super Bowl, or ahem, getting your manuscript accepted by a prestigious publishing house are all positive events. Reflecting on them will probably bring a smile to your face but thanks to habituation that smile wanes with each passing day. This is the double bind gratefulness finds itself in. You can only be grateful for something you're familiar with. But being grateful for it makes the familiar *more* familiar, thus accelerating the effects of habituation.

You can try making a list of things you're grateful for but you'll soon find out that it too tends to make you more familiar with the familiar and, oh dear, there you are back in the soup of habituation. Studies have found that practicing gratitude is most effective when you haven't habituated to the positive event (you just got a publishing contract!) and slopes down to almost nothing the more adapted you become to it (six months passed since you signed the contract).

In many ways, practicing gratitude is like taking a drug that loses its potency the more you use it. Is there no way to make gratitude powerful AND long lasting?

Radical Gratitude: A Proven Way To Make Appreciation Work

Practicing gratitude for the *presence* of something binds us to the law of habituation, but what if we switched the frame and concentrated on its *absence*? In others words, replace "*I'm so happy to have Dave in my life!*" with "*Imagine if I had never met Dave?*" Replace "*I'm thrilled that Publishers Weekly gave my book a good review*" with "*What if Publishers Weekly didn't review my book?*"

This is the provocative idea put forth by psychologists who

champion "counterfactual reasoning" as an effective way of practicing gratitude. Counterfactual thinking is a concept in psychology that involves creating possible alternatives to life events that have already occurred—something contrary to what actually happened. They are marked by questions like "What if..." and "If only..."

Counterfactual thinking can create negative emotions like regret ("If only I accepted that paltry advance because now nobody else wants the book!") or positive ones like relief ("What if I hadn't accepted that paltry advance? I'd have nothing!').

As it happens, some of the most cutting edge research on gratitude uses counterfactual reasoning and surprise! The results have tended toward the stellar. For example, in one study, subjects who wrote about how they might *never* have met their romantic partner were more satisfied with their relationship than were those who wrote about how they *did* meet their partner.

Researchers believe that counterfactual thinking works by jarringly 'unadapting' yourself to positive events you've habituated to. Many psychologists call it the "George Bailey Effect" after the greatest—though fictional—example of its success—the 1946 Frank Capra film *It's a Wonderful Life*.

In the movie an angel takes a suicidal man named George Bailey on a tour of the world as if he had never been born. Instead of asking George to count his blessings, the angel invites him to observe a world in which those blessings never materialized. The exercise jolts George Bailey into an emotional reckoning which instantly cures his depression. Research suggests that the movie was onto something. Counterfactual reasoning can turn the familiar into a surprise, a sure way of "unadapting" to habituation, at least temporarily.

Even though the concept of counterfactual thinking goes back to Plato it's only in the last few years that researchers have begun to study its effects on gratitude. That's because mentally undoing events is something we typically apply to *negative*, not positive events. It's natural to think counterfactually when things go wrong ("What if I hadn't been texting? I wouldn't have hit the car in front of me"). Put simply, it never occurred to psychologists that "mentally undoing a positive event" would have the counter-intuitive effect of making you more grateful for it.

How Writers Can Get The Most Out Of Counterfactual Reasoning

The single most effective way writers can create the "George Bailey effect" is to visualize a counterfactual experience in the most vivid, *believable* way. Let's take the example of what many of my successful midlister friends consider a rejection—getting a good but not starred review in Publishers Weekly.

Whoa, whoa, whoa. How is getting a good review in Publishers Weekly a rejection? Most of us would crawl through the veins of a blue whale to get one. Well, if you've never been reviewed by PW it certainly isn't a rejection. But if three of your books have and the fourth doesn't get a starred review you can start feeling like the industry thinks you're good but not great. Also, your brain is wired to perceive it as an inability to get into a tribe (in this case a prestigious one that commands respect and likely to give you more resources), and therefore a threat to your survival.

At any rate, this is the exactly the kind of rejection that gratitude is so effective at neutralizing because it can help you focus on the good that you got rather than the good that you didn't.

So let's begin. Let's say you're working under an editor whose authors regularly get starred reviews but YOU didn't. Yours was positive enough to lift a blurb and put it on the cover of your book but the reviewer didn't think it was outstanding enough to warrant stars. You're gutted because in your mind this marks you as one of your editor's inferior writers. Sit down, close your eyes and get ready to test drive your first act of radical gratitude. I want you to visualize the following:

You get a certified letter in the mail from Publishers Weekly.

It says, "Dear Author, we regret to inform you that we've retracted the review we made of your book in Publishers Weekly. Our book editor reviewed a very similar book and mistakenly labeled it as yours. In fact, nobody at Publishers Weekly reviewed your book and we have no plans to do so. We will be printing a retraction next week. We are copying your editor and agent on this fact."

Five minutes later you get an email from your editor.

It says, "OMG! We've already gone to press with the PW blurb on the cover! This is going to cost us thousands of dollars to undo!"

Five minutes later your agent calls.

He says, "WTF! Do you know what this is going to do to your reputation?!"

You call friends and family to tell them what happened.

You've told everyone about the PW review. Everyone. And now you're going to have to untell them. You've gone from getting a solid review to being told your book wasn't worth reviewing. How will you relate the story? Will you tell people that PW never intended to review your book? How embarrassed are you at telling the story? What are you thinking? What are you feeling?

A week later the publisher sends you two copies of the book.

You hold them side-by-side. The old version prominently displays the PW blurb on the top of the cover. It's gone from the new cover. Wiped out. And you're startled at how much more enticing the cover is with the blurb than without it.

...

Question: How grateful are you now for the solid, but unstarred Publishers Weekly review? My guess is that like George Bailey in *It's A Wonderful Life*, you are overwhelmed with gratitude.

You can apply the power of counterfactual reasoning to anything you want to appreciate more deeply. Just remember that to get the maximum effect you must VIVIDLY imagine not just the absence of it but the specific and believable way it could be taken away from you.

Gratitude is the gateway drug to positive emotions like love, safety, joy, serenity and determination. Cultivating it on a regular basis improves our attitude towards writing and makes us more resilient. But in order to make it work we have to 'unadapt' to the habituation that familiarity can bring, so use counterfactual reasoning regularly. It works.

Ask George Bailey.

Chapter Thirteen

Maintaining A Bulletproof Future

Early in my writing career I realized processing rejection was just as important as producing manuscripts. I had a sense of clarity that my writer friends—the ones with more talent, the ones felled by constant rejection—did not. We all went to writing retreats to hone our craft, but I also went to research libraries to hone my mind. I had an intuitive sense that talent alone was not the only factor to success.

Do you know what taught me that? Tennis.

I used to play competitively and as a kid I noticed something odd: The most talented players didn't always win. I particularly remember one guy, a friend, who'd kick my butt in practice and then lose to me in a tournament. Why? Because he mentally collapsed when a lesser player like me won a few games. He wasn't mentally tough. He wasn't resilient. He couldn't get over his setbacks.

This taught me a valuable lesson that served me in my writing career: Talent isn't enough. I needed a lot more than a literary skill set to succeed as a writer. I needed to cultivate both talent *and* resiliency.

I am an anomaly in writing. I'm one of the 1,400 out of 250,000 authors in the U.S. who make a good living as a writer. If you read my body of work there is no way you would conclude I swim in the deep end of the talent pool. I am at best, slightly above average. I'm a living, walking example of Dean Simonton's conclusion—that once you meet a minimum level of talent, success goes to the person with the highest threshold for failure. In other words, grit. Resiliency. Resolve. The kind you get by developing a coping strategy that turns poison into medicine.

This is my message to you: If I, almost undoubtedly less talented than you, can make it by developing a bulletproof consciousness, then you can too. Reading this book is a great start to making that possible, but it's just a start. The real work begins when you come back to the book over and over as you experience the disorienting rejections you will face in the future.

Break This Glass During An Emergency

One of the problems of dipping back into a book for a refresher is that it's often hard to remember where you saw that useful concept or effective exercise. To solve that problem I've created an appendix that lists all the issues, concepts, exercises, and insights with their corresponding page numbers.

Think of it as a kind emotional EpiPen. The next time you suffer a rejection-induced pain just break the appendix open and inject the right chapter straight into your thigh.

In the meantime, I want to go over some of the key concepts I've discussed, but instead of simply rehashing them I'm going to tell you which ones I personally find most valuable. I also want to do it as a case study, using a painful rejection I recently suffered: I sent my agent the manuscript to an advice book I thought would do really well. My agent refused to take it on even though I'm a subject matter expert with a fair amount of successful books in the genre. *"Your last book on that subject tanked,"* she said rather directly, *"And publishers will not be able to see past that to consider your manuscript on its own merits."*

I had to process a couple of pain points—that my agent didn't have enough faith to take the fight on, that publishers wouldn't consider my work on the basis of one failure, and that my hopes for the book were utterly crushed. No verse to add to the great play. No flowers to gift. Just a cutting sense of embarrassment that as a veteran writer of fourteen years I still had to face this kind of crap.

Here is how I used the concepts in this book to process the rejection:

Fact: My Brain Is Wired For Negativity

I get clear that my initial alarmist response to the rejection isn't a character flaw—it's a structural feature of my brain. This wiring naturally perceives social rejection (an agent/editor rejecting my manuscript) as a physical threat that doesn't respond to logic and reason. My conscious mind may treat it appropriately ("What a bummer!") but my brain greets it with a Defcon 1 alarm ("I'm being cast out of the tribe!").

Short term, I connect with my various tribes knowing it's the best way to calm a brain highjacked by alarm. For example, I had lunch with my sister, a successful historical fiction novelist who's had her own share of rejection horror stories. I always come away from our talks feeling loved and part of a "tribe," countering my brain's propensity for believing that I'm not. Once I accomplish that goal, I think about insights that might sustain me.

Insight: Publishing Systematically Rejects Its Most Talented People.

I remind myself of publishing's perversity because it helps put my rejection in context. I imagined former Apple CEO Steve Jobs' "agent" telling him that Verizon would not consider the iPhone on its merits because the Apple III was a failure. This kind of rejection would never happen in other industries, but it happens regularly in publishing. I also extended the absurdity by picturing publishing's gatekeepers as hapless dyslexics who storm into a bank and yell, *"Air in the hands, motherstickers!! This is a fuck up!"*

I Ask Myself: Was The Rejection An Indictment Of My Work?

This is the existential question most of us writers find ourselves asking—are we getting rejected because we're no good or because of other factors beyond our control? I realized in this case the rejection wasn't an indictment of my talent; it was an indictment of a skittish, shortsighted industry.

Insight: Get Clear On Why I Write

I don't write to get a publisher's blessing. I write because I like to tell stories, help people solve problems and maybe even make them laugh a little. I write to add a verse to Whitman's powerful play. I know I have something to say and I know there are people who need to hear it. My agent/publishers erected a wall between us but I concentrate on my purpose and know that if I'm strategic —and patient—I can figure out how to scale it and deliver my flowers.

Fact: The Defining Characteristic Of Success Is A High Threshold For Failure

I remind myself that people who fail the most tend to succeed the most. I remind myself that I have suffered a long, LONG line of rejections and this is just the latest and not even close to being the worst. Just because I don't know what to do about it right now doesn't mean I won't in the future. For now, I take comfort that this particular rejection and the way I react to it, is part of a lifelong process of building higher and higher thresholds for failure.

Fact: Successful People Treat Failure As "Empowered Attributionists"

I don't see my rejections as blessings in disguise; they are terrible no good very bad things. And I treat them as such. But I ask myself: Is this failure malleable or immutable? If I believe it's immutable ("there's nothing I can do about this") then I'm powerless to affect change. If it's malleable ("Maybe I ought to consider self-publishing this book") then I have some agency to make more attempts, which is the defining characteristic of successful people.

Insight: I Must Manage The Pain Of Rejection, Not Pretend It Doesn't Hurt

I follow the steps I outlined in Chapter Five:

1. Feel my feelings
I know if I don't they'll come back to haunt me.

2. Institute The 48 Hour Sulking Rule
I know that unending feelings can cause as much damage as unfelt feelings.

3. Go THROUGH The Negative Not Around It
Sometimes I prefer using the "extinction" exercise in Chapter Five but "Watching The Weather" seemed more appropriate for this type of rejection so here's what I did:

> I pictured a cloudless blue sky taken over by the dark clouds of my agent's response and the publishing industry's refusal to consider my manuscript. I let the clouds do whatever they want to do—turn gray, black, storm, thunder, hail and snow. I just observe. Accept. I don't resist. I don't try to change the clouds. I don't make them lighter or visualize them going away. The bulletproof consciousness does not try to control the weather; it responds to it in the moment (galoshes anyone?). Slowly, with enough time, the clouds go away on their own and I'm left with blue sky. I use the short meditation not to feel motivated for the battle ahead or provide some false sense of positivity, but as a way to ground myself, to "clear" the air, get a higher level of thinking around the

rejection, and connect to the great truth of emotional pain: That this too shall pass.

Insight: Distancing and Distraction Are Powerful Analgesics

I didn't obsess about this particular rejection but I still used the tools that best resolve rumination because I find them so effective: Distancing and Distraction. For example, I chose to "watch" a fictional documentary of the rejection. The "narrator" interviewed editors and publishers who said things like, "It's true, we are most likely not going to look at the manuscript if Michael's previous book didn't do well." This made me realize that my agent wasn't expressing a lack of confidence in my manuscript (which angered me) as much as reflecting the industry's mentality. The anger and resentment toward my agent receded and I was left in a more peaceful frame of mind.

ACTION: Inoculate Myself Against Future Rejections By Building Beneficial Neural Networks

This doesn't help me deal with any one specific rejection but over time it has dramatically lessened the pain of all rejections because I've consciously "rewired" my brain to make the positive stick more like Velcro than Teflon. I highly encourage you to check out neuropsychologist Rick Hanson's book, *Hardwiring Happiness*, to get more details. Basically he suggests we consciously mimic the strategies our built-in negative bias uses by doing the following:

1. Scan for the positive

I'm not talking about looking for a "silver lining" but of seeking out the all-out, 100% genuinely positive. In my case it was the lunch I had with my sister. She can make me feel like a million bucks—after taxes. I also scan for small wins. For example, the day my agent said NO, I got a five-star review on Amazon for one of my other books. Not exactly earth-shattering news but I've learned that scanning for the positive trains my brain to be as sensitive to the empowering as it is to the disempowering.

2. Treat The Positive With The Intensity You Treat The Negative

What do you do after somebody important in your life—like my sister—makes you feel better about a rejection? You move on. Don't. That's your brain minimizing the positive. After lunch with my sister I made it a point to fully absorb the positive feelings of belonging, of feeling understood, of being loved. After she left, I closed my eyes and "regenerated" those feelings not just because they felt good but for the express purpose of building a more positive neural network. I make it my business to treat the positive with the same intensity my brain treats the negative.

For example, if you get a good review on Amazon, don't just scan it. Read every word. Dwell on it. Read it twice. Analyze it. Imagine the consequences. Absorb and celebrate the positive now not later as current experiences and emotions, not recalled memories, build stronger neural networks. "Absorb" the positive experience for about 30 seconds, as that's how long it takes for neurons to "fire and wire."

One More Conclusion To Hammer In

A bulletproof consciousness isn't a costume you slip on once and parade down the street daring someone to reject you. You grow it from the inside out. You cultivate it until it becomes second nature. You train it with repetition.

Always return to the central, driving motivation for why you write, for it is only there that you can find comfort and peace. You write, if I may be bold enough to point out, to express your thoughts, communicate your feelings and release your imagination. You write to voice your passions, to provide value for other people, to gift humanity with the flowers of possibility.

But mostly, you write for the same reason painters paint, sculptors sculpt, architects design and builders build: That insatiable, inescapable but wondrous need to create. And that need doesn't come with the asterisk of outcome. Picasso never thought, "I'm only going to paint if I can be successful." Shakespeare didn't say, "I'm only going to write if millions read my work."

Be true to your nature as a creative being: Create without regard to the results.

Appendix

Exercises

Other Books By Michael Alvear

**"Three hat tips to Make A Killing
On Kindle!"**
—*Guy Kawasaki*, Entrepreneurial
bestseller in his book, *APE*.

**"I insist that all my clients read this
book before they publish—and I have
thousands of clients."**—*Kimberly
Hitchens*, Owner www.booknook.biz,
an Amazon-preferred ebook conversion
specialist.

**This Book Will Save You From The Time Sucking, No-
Value Vortex Of Blogging, Facebook and Twitter.** I will show
you convincing industry research that social media is the least
effective way to sell books on Kindle. And then I'll show you how
to:

- Rank On Page 1 Of Amazon's Search Engine

- Come up with must-click book titles.

- Pick the right categories.

- Pick from five of the most effective launch prices.

- Get reviews that make people want to buy your book.

- Use the Look Inside Feature to sell more books on
  Kindle.

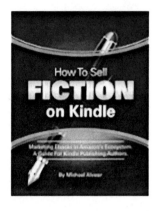

This Guide Answers The Most Critical Question You Face As A Fiction Writer: *What keyword phrases should I use for my novel?*

I'm not going to show you how to find them. I'm going to <u>tell you what they are</u>. This book is quite literally an encyclopedia of keyword phrases that buyers type into Amazon's search engine when they try to find books in your genre. It's your biggest challenge answered: Discoverability.

Every Book Buyer Goes Through Nine Decision Points On Their Way To A Purchase.

Will they click on your cover? Read your book description? Click on "Look Inside"? Wince at your price? Read your reviews? I'm going to show you how you can influence each of the nine decision points so they result in a sale.